THE STORY OF MONEY

THE STORY OF MONEY

The Journey From Shells and Shekels to Bills and Bitcoin

SEAN COVER

ISBN: 978-1-7373416-0-4 (*paperback*)
ISBN: 978-1-7373416-2-8 (*hardcover*)

DEDICATION

*Thank you to the friends and family
that have supported me along the way.*

TABLE OF
CONTENTS

THE ROLE OF MONEY

F OR MOST OF us, money is a means to an end. It is a tool that allows us to buy what we want. To get money, though, we have to work for it. It is an endless loop—go to work, get paid, buy goods and services, and start again. People tend not to consider the system's mechanics, the "how" and the "why" of money. These things are essential to understand, however. Money is the most important tool that humans have invented—one that has allowed us to progress as a species far beyond what all other animals on the planet have accomplished. Money is a universal language, the language of value.

Nearly all Americans take the dollar for granted. Across the world, it is not a given to have a relatively stable currency, far from it. Human history with money is defined by failure, where currencies collapsed very frequently. Even today, America's stable dollar is not the norm; it is the exception. While those of us in the world's wealthiest countries only think about other dominant currencies, such as the euro, pound, yen, and renminbi, the rest of the world is not as fortunate.

For the five billion people—the majority of all humans— who live outside of the US, Europe, China, and Japan, stable money is not something that can be relied on and expected. While in the United States we fight over how much to tax and distribute our riches, Lebanon experienced a hyperinflation event in 2020, with a 112.4% increase in consumer prices between July 2019 and July 2020.[1] The currency itself cannot be depended on for these people, making it impossible to store wealth throughout years and decades.

WHY MONEY MATTERS

WHEN ASKED THE question, "What is money?" it is not uncommon to hear that it is a tool that humans use to determine value and exchange for other goods, but any further questioning tends to leave people stumped. They cannot answer the question, "What separates good money from bad money?" or even "How does our system of money work?"

As it turns out, the answers to these questions are crucial to understanding society today. Yes, money allows us to trade with one another and value goods and services, but it does much more than that. Money is the base layer on which the entirety of human civilization is built. All human coordination relies on the language of value; without money, great societies would not have been built. It is not a coincidence that the most remarkable civilizations throughout history, such as ancient Rome and Greece, had strong currencies for their periods that were utilized to build empires that remained dominant for hundreds of years.

But why *should* people in countries like the US or England bother to learn about money? If the currency is stable, then what is the point?

Without most of us realizing it, a significant shift in how modern money works is occurring. It has been happening for the last fifty years, but only in the last decade has the growth accelerated. This change in how money works— meaning the process in which new currency enters the economy and the checks and balances of that process to keep the system working—has resulted in numerous societal changes that are not immediately apparent. Because money is the base layer of our society, its effects on our institutions are profound. These influences are vast and range from the increasing cost of college tuition and healthcare to the rise in inequality between the wealthy and the poor. The root of these problems and many more all trace back to our system of money itself. Instead of recognizing this though, we debate these issues with a narrow lens, without realizing that the real problem often lies in how money works. Only by understanding how our money truly functions can we consider good reforms to many of our institutions.

Money is both simple and complicated. When considering it on its own, it seems obvious—money is a way to transfer value. Yet digging into the particulars reveals the many ways in which using a simple tool like money can lead to endless complications, contradictions, and headaches.

When considering the question posed earlier, "What separates good money from bad money?" most people would be at a loss, likely defaulting to the idea that good money needs to be accepted in many stores. That gets the answer precisely backwards. Being commonly accepted is not what makes a form of money good; it is the reverse. Sound money naturally finds its way to being widely accepted.

Remember, up until 1971 the United States was on a gold standard, meaning that the number of dollars in circulation was limited by the amount of gold a bank held in its reserves.

Think about what this really means. When the US was on its gold standard, gold was the true currency of the nation. While dollars existed in name and on paper, dollars were simply a paper proxy for a certain amount of gold. Since the dollar has been a representation of gold for much of its life, the dollar as we know it today is a young currency, brand new in terms of global monetary history. With no gold backing its value, the dollar is still new, and alongside its rise over the last half-century, many societal problems have emerged.

Yet, our understanding of how the dollar works is still limited. While many are aware that the Federal Reserve is predominantly in charge of new dollar issuance, the "how" and "why" of the currency creation process is unknown to all but a few Americans. This lack of understanding is compounded further because money as a system is not taught in schools. We have no knowledge of money's past and the impact that it has had on countless human societies.

In many ways, money is humanity's most important invention. Money allows us to trade efficiently, measure value, and, most importantly, save wealth throughout time. These traits enable us to create the rules, institutions, and society that we now call America. Consider an analogy of our country as a tree. The branches of the tree represent institutions, such as our healthcare and education systems. Our system of money is not another branch in this example. Instead, it is the roots of the tree that allow it to grow.

For much of history and through the first few thousand years of monetary history, money could not store value for any length of time. Primitive money functioned much in the way that electricity works today. If the electricity is not utilized right away, it cannot easily be saved for later. Use it or lose it. The same was true of money; if it did not get spent quickly, it would rapidly become worthless.

The advent of money allowed humans to store value throughout the years, which resulted in countless advancements in science, literature, mathematics, and much more. *The Story of Money* will explain how good money is an absolute necessity for a thriving economy and how it is impossible to achieve one without it.

We will start by dissecting money itself. What is money? What are its purposes and properties? From there we will learn about the history of money and the long journey that has taken us from where money started to where it is today. Understanding the history of money provides an essential background for understanding how our modern system of money operates. There are many lessons to be learned from money's history. After analyzing our current system of money and the societal problems resulting from it, we will look into how money is changing and what the future of money will look like.

Let us get started.

WHAT IS MONEY?

MONEY IS A tool of exchange. It is a way for people to value goods, services, and wealth in a standard measurement. You go to a store and see that a plastic drinking cup is priced at $5, while the glass mug next to it is $10. It is not that those items are worth a certain amount of paper cash, because modern money has no actual worth in and of itself. What the dollar—and money in general—allows us to do is make a comparison where we can now say "two plastic cups have the same value as one glass mug."

Money allows us to measure value and transfer it through both space and time. Moving value through space means, as it sounds, that you can exchange value in various locations away from where the money was earned. Transferring value through time means that in the future you will still have your value. Ten dollars of value today is equal to ten dollars of value one week from now. Of course, as we will see, transferring value throughout time is not as easy as one would believe.

Money has three main functions.

1. Unit of account
2. Medium of exchange
3. Store of value

Each of these functions has a different purpose and, as we will see throughout the book, various forms of money succeed and fail at different levels with these three functions.

The first function of money is to be a *unit of account*. A unit of account is when the goods and services available in a country or region are priced using the same form of money. This is the property of money that you might be most familiar with. In the United States, the dollar is the only true unit of account. When you walk into a store or shop online, everything that you see is priced in dollars.

Functioning as a unit of account allows users to compare one thing against another in a common measurement easily. It also allows users to compare prices over time. If my rent in 2019 was $1,600 and now it is $1,700, I understand exactly how much my rent increased. While being a unit of account is often the first function of money that comes to mind, it is the least important one in determining the long-term success of a money, for reasons that will be discussed shortly.

The second function of money is to be a *medium of exchange*. A medium of exchange refers to being the actual tool used in a trade for goods and services. Many different forms of money and commodities can function as a medium of exchange for a given transaction. Let us say that I help my friend move into a new apartment. In return for helping him move, that friend agrees to provide me with a case of beer.

In that example, the beer is functioning as the medium of exchange, or the money, in that transaction.

What makes a suitable medium of exchange? A medium of exchange should be common and accessible, have a constant utility, be easily recognizable, and be resistant to counterfeiting.

The final of the big three functions of money is being a *store of value*. A store of value refers to an asset that maintains its value over time without depreciating. Being able to save money over a long period is a crucial need for an economically healthy population. A good store of value will allow its owner to sell or exchange it at a future date for a similar or higher purchasing power than initially acquired.

In most of the world's economies, the local currency is often relied on as a store of value. The US dollar, euro, Japanese yen, Swiss franc, and Singapore dollar have been among the most stable currencies in recent times. However, national currencies can fail as a store of value when hyperinflation occurs. The reality for much of the world, which does not have access to the previously listed currencies, is that it is challenging to store wealth over time. These people are instead forced to use unreliable and rapidly depreciating currencies. Having access to the US dollar is a privilege that is often taken for granted by those who have never experienced living with less reliable currencies.

In those instances where national currencies experience high inflation, assets such as gold, silver, real estate, and even fine art have functioned as stores of value throughout history. While these items' relative value does fluctuate over time, they have maintained value throughout history because they all share specific properties, namely that the supply of these items is limited. The supply of a good store of value cannot easily be increased, as opposed to a poorly managed national currency. A base level of demand combined with a limited supply makes for the best stores of value.

Most of us may give only a passing thought to the function of money on a daily basis, but the store of value is money's most important property. Many things can be easily transferred and function as a medium of exchange or unit of account. Why were gold and silver used as money for thousands of years when almost any metal could be transferred equally well? It is because gold and silver allowed the societies that used them to best store wealth over time.

While the instinct is to define money as something that is accepted in stores and in which prices are denominated, this is again backwards. For shops to desire a currency, the money must first be capable of holding value. It is holding value throughout time that causes a form of money to be desired in the first place. Once the store of value function is realized, a money becomes gradually more accepted in daily transactions. Money must first store value before it can function as a generally accepted medium of exchange and finally be a unit of account. Without being a store of value, there is no long-term planning, since all money acquired would need to immediately be spent before it lost value.

In jurisdictions where high inflation is commonplace, the local currency is still relied on as a store of value. Unfortunately, it does not work well. Their people are forced to use these bad forms of money—the failing national currencies—because there are no other options. Either oppressive capital controls by governments restrict them from using better currencies, or they simply do not have access to more stable currencies like the dollar. It is worth noting, people in these countries would jump at the chance to exchange their local currencies for dollars—not because the dollar is any better at being a unit of account or medium of exchange, but because the dollar is much better at storing value.

Besides the three functions of money, good money also has certain fundamental properties. These properties are divisibility, durability, portability, recognizability, and scarcity. Various forms of money are better at certain of these traits than others. There are always trade-offs.

Divisibility is necessary because money needs to be used for both large and small transactions. If a form of money is not sufficiently divisible, it cannot be used to make small purchases. Divisibility goes hand-in-hand with scarcity, since scarcity is often the biggest determinant of the value of a money. For example, gold has long been considered more valuable than silver, yet for most of monetary history, silver was the more dominant money. This was because gold was actually too valuable and not divisible enough to function well for many transactions. Money must be able to be divided into small enough portions to work for small purchases.

Durability and portability are self-explanatory. A currency needs to be able to withstand day-to-day use and be able to be easily transported from one location to another. A flower cannot function as money because it would fall apart within days or weeks.

Recognizability ensures that people know what money is. Modern money is standardized. We understand what dollar bills look like, and we know that they are money. Money should be consistent and easily identified as currency. This need for clarity is why the US has one president on its different denominations of currency. If hundreds of different faces were on $1 bills, there would be increased confusion as to whether the money was legitimate or not.

Finally, scarcity has already been explained as a part of

the definition for a store of value. Without some level of scarcity, a form of money cannot hold its value over time.

Now that we have defined what money is, we will go back to explore the history of money and how different monetary systems have evolved over time and through to today. We are going to use the properties and functions of money that we discussed here to analyze other monetary systems and determine in which areas they succeed and where they fail.

A key theme throughout the remainder of *The Story of Money* will be trade-offs. As mentioned earlier, there are always trade-offs. A particular type of money or system might excel in some areas but lack in others, while a different form of money may have the opposite features. Once we learn and understand the lessons from monetary history, we will thoroughly explore the modern system of money and how it has more of these trade-offs than most of us realize.

PART I:
THE HISTORY OF MONEY

MONEY ALWAYS DEVELOPS

MONEY HAS ALWAYS existed in human civilizations of meaningful size. As soon as humans became capable of grouping and communicating with one another, the need to trade inevitably arose. This need to exchange goods or services between humans is the driving force behind the existence of money. The goods that fulfilled the role of money in early groups of people were not merely chosen to be money by leaders in the way that we think of today with the US government minting the US dollar. Instead, the items that eventually functioned as money had certain traits that allowed them to be superior forms of money to other goods.

As we will see, while some goods work well as money, most do not. To elaborate on this further, we must first imagine what a society would be like if there were no such thing as money. We will discuss two types of non-money cultures: gift economies and barter systems.

GIFT ECONOMIES

A GIFT ECONOMY is a system where the basis of trade typically occurs in the context of interpersonal relationships and promises. Instead of always needing to trade one good for another, individuals in a gift economy ask their friends for required items. Instead of paying for the goods with money, the receiver of the good may help the giver friend in the future with a similar type of favor. While it would seem that gift societies must be more generous than we are used to today, gift societies resulted in the same struggle over power dynamics that we see in any other economic system.

First, gift economies require abundance to function. Successful gift cultures arose in populations that typically lived in locations with moderate climates and abundant food. This type of environment allowed all members of a society to produce enough to survive, while giving and receiving gifts to acquire whatever they were missing. When goods are scarce, people do not want to part with their items and will not merely give them away for free. When scarcity becomes an issue, gift economies dissolve, and barter and money naturally arise.

The second issue that inescapably arose in any gift culture was that the act of giving would eventually become political. Profit in a culture of gift exchange did not have to be a profit of money. Instead, those who gave gifts abundantly could achieve power through social relationships, influence, and prestige. The focus on gift exchange turns every act of "kindness" into a careful investment. It often became custom that once you gave a gift to someone, they would be obligated to repay you with a gift of their own in the future. Because of this, people in a particular tribe or culture would begin to specifically plan to whom to give gifts to with the knowledge that the receiving person would have to give them something in return. As a result, gift economies often end up as debt societies, where the politics of gift obligations lord over all.

THE BARTER SYSTEM

THE TERM "BARTER" describes situations or communities

where one good is directly traded for another. In a system where there is no actual money used, the only way for any kind of exchange to occur is to trade one good for another directly. If a farmer wants to sell chickens to a blacksmith in exchange for spears, the farmer and the blacksmith need to agree on how many chickens equal how many spears. A barter society would, in theory, extend to an entire group of people, all trading item-for-item depending on what they have and what they need.

This construct has many issues and does not work at scale. Without a standard measure of value—a form of money—it is impossible for communities to obtain a consistent value for a good or service.

What if, when the farmer approaches the blacksmith, the blacksmith desires jewelry instead of chickens? The farmer would not be able to make the exchange unless he first goes to the jeweler and attempts to trade chickens for jewelry. Once a group of people exceeds more than a dozen or two in size, trying to track and coordinate which person desires which item becomes impossible. The reliance on the two parties in a trade both needing the other's good is known as a "double coincidence of wants."

Barter also fails as a system due to a lack of divisibility. Many goods cannot be easily divided and therefore cannot be traded for particular items. If a farmer only has one chicken, yet the blacksmith requires two chickens in exchange for a spear, there is no way for the sale to proceed since neither individual's units—chickens nor spears—are divisible.

Beyond the double coincidence of wants and the issue of divisibility, it is nearly impossible to store wealth over time in a barter system. Many goods either spoil or have a limited shelf life, which prevents the ability to store value. An apple farmer has no way to save their apples from year to year. The inability to save presents a significant problem with barter, as well as many early forms of money, as yields of a commodity could vary significantly in any given year. With barter, there is no such thing as savings for most people. One must exchange his goods before they spoil.

If these criticisms of barter are correct—and they are—how did societies manage to get anything done? In actuality, there are no records of any society that traded exclusively through barter. Does this mean that all you have heard about the history of barter is a myth, nothing more than lies and tall tales? No, it does not. Barter was used quite often in early societies. What begins as barter, though, quickly turns to money.

As discussed, barter fails due to its reliance on the double coincidence of wants, which does not work in a society of meaningful size. Too many situations arise where two transacting people do not desire the other person's good and they need to seek a third good to satisfy an individual's needs. The result inevitably leads to a local economy where people spend more time trying to acquire goods that they can use specifically for trading, rather than acquiring goods that they themselves need. In other words, people would spend much of their time seeking out the goods most desired by other people, specifically with the intent to trade them away again in the future.

The benefits of this type of indirect exchange—acquiring goods that you may not need in order to trade them away in the future—are so apparent that the practice would begin almost immediately in a system of barter. It is a simple reality that certain goods are always more widely desired than others. As all community members gradually realize the importance of acquiring certain goods solely for trading again in the future, those goods would see their desirability rise even further as demand for them increased. Eventually, most trades would be conducted using only a few commonly accepted goods. These goods are, in essence, money.

While there may not have been thriving economies solely operating through barter systems the way many of us imagined, discussing barter allows us to conceptualize and understand the need for money. Even when a society begins without an established form of money, money will inevitably arise.

When studying great ancient civilizations, their successful monetary systems are often ignored. We admire the buildings and the advancements in science, while neglecting the monetary structure's role in allowing that society to thrive in the first place. Indeed, societies that adopted better forms of money than their contemporaries have consistently innovated, succeeded, and prospered. This oversight is understandable, as our modern system of money is also taken for granted. The reality is that up until recent history, most forms of money failed quickly. In fact, the difference between using a good type of money and a bad form of money was often the differentiating factor in whether a society succeeded or failed.

THE FIRST FORMS OF MONEY

W HILE MONEY HAS always existed in settled human societies, detailed records of it have not. In our modern Homo sapiens form, humans have existed for approximately 200,000 years, yet the first records of money only date as recently as about 9000 BCE. This relatively recent date means that using money has only been part of human history for 3.7% of our life as a species. If that is the case, what happened around 9000 BCE that provoked a change from the previous 96.3% of our existence?

The key demarcation point, the occurrence that separates humanity's history with money into clear "before" and "after" periods, was the development of agriculture. While wild grains have been eaten for over 100,000 years, true domestication and modern farming techniques did not begin until around 9500 BCE. Around this time, eight crops, known as the Neolithic founder crops, began to be cultivated.[2] These crops—barley, bitter vetch, chickpeas, emmer wheat, einkorn wheat, flax, lentils, and peas—were grown in the Levant region, which stretched from northeast Egypt into the Middle East.

AGRARIANISM PRECEDES MONEY

BEFORE THE DEVELOPMENT of agriculture, humans lived a much more nomadic lifestyle. They hunted for animals and foraged for plant foods. Hunter-gatherer societies were typically relatively small, with even the most prominent groups rarely exceeding one hundred members.[3] Since food needed to be found or hunted, meals were not guaranteed. Even though many hunter-gatherer societies were quite successful and well fed, the foraging lifestyle required the group to rely on each other in a somewhat egalitarian way. Since resources were limited, groups needed to remain small in size.

Once the development of agriculture began and the domestication of crops became commonplace, the way humans lived shifted drastically. Since crops were now being farmed, humans could live in one stable location while still being able to secure food. Population sizes started to grow significantly and people became less dependent on the group's success as a whole.

Since farmers were limited in the crops they could grow on any one farm, crop specialization began to occur and yields were grown at previously unachievable levels. There was more food than ever before, and farmers had more food than was needed to feed their families. Since farmers were producing more food than was necessary, combined with the fact that farmers could not grow every desirable crop themselves with their specialized farms, the growth of trade skyrocketed. And what is essential to the development of trade? The need for money.

As population sizes continued to grow alongside agricultural development, the evolution of money became necessary for trade. As discussed while examining barter, certain goods were acquired to be used explicitly for trading again in the future. The goods that took on this quality, becoming money for their societies, tended to be goods that a group's members almost universally desired and possessed in relative abundance. This type of money is known as "commodity money"—when a good that already has value takes on an additional monetary role.

Throughout this period and continuing through the next few thousand years, multiple forms of money continued to emerge. While livestock and plant products often became money, shells, beads, and many other commodities were used by various societies. While these goods worked in their primitive monetary role, none of these items were particularly good forms of money. For this reason, most goods eventually fail at being money.

At its core, money is a neutral tool. It allows us to exchange goods and services using a standard unit for valuation. Money does not take sides, nor is it supposed to be easily manipulated. For a form of money to succeed, it needs to maintain a delicate balance between scarcity and abundance. If a valuable good is too limited in supply, for example, if only a handful of rare gems existed among a tribe, the gems would fail as money because there is not enough of them to conduct trade at scale.

On the other hand, a commodity will also fail at being money if it is too plentiful. If a society used sunflowers as their money, but there are numerous sunflower fields right outside the village, the money will fail due to overabundance. Money that exists in excess is trivial to acquire and is susceptible to supply manipulation, control, and devaluation from the lack of scarcity.

To study humanity's history with money is to observe our species as we have searched for the magic bowl of Goldilocks' money. The ideal money must balance between being not too scarce but not overly abundant either. This search has been a 12,000-year march of progress, and we have not entirely solved it yet.

To understand this journey, we must ask: What separates

good money from bad money? What has worked through-out history? What has not?

THE MALDIVES' COWRIE SHELLS

ONE OF THE most important examples of a successful and long-lasting pre-coinage money is the cowrie shell. Cowries were the shells of a specific type of mollusk—sea snails—and have a distinct ovular shape and appearance. The evidence of cowrie shells' use as money dates to the very beginnings of money in parts of ancient China.[4] Over the course of thousands of years, the use of cowrie shells spread across Asia, Africa, and even parts of Europe.

What made the cowrie so successful was how it excelled in many of the properties of money. Cowries were easily identifiable and difficult to counterfeit. They looked unique enough that buyers and sellers did not have to be overly concerned by the prospect of potentially receiving fake cowries in the form of a different type of shell. Cowries were also relatively small in size and light in weight—unlike later metals—which allowed them to be easily transported and used in transactions both small and large. Importantly, cowries were also quite durable, enabling them to be used over long periods and allowing families to pass wealth to their children over generations.

Finally, cowrie shells were scarce enough to retain worth and fulfill the store of value property of money. Cowries are most abundantly found in the waters of the Indian Ocean and were predominantly collected in the Maldive Islands. This means that the use of cowrie shells as money was only spread through trade and travel. It is quite incredible, then, to realize the reach that the cowrie managed to achieve. Since cowries' supply was so geographically limited, it was impossible for users of cowries located at great distances to over-inflate the currency. One could not simply go to the nearest body of water hoping to find cowries. This supply limit allowed for a degree of scarcity that was uncommon in primitive forms of money. As a result, cowries tended to be valued higher in societies the further away they were from the Maldives.

The combination of monetary properties in which the cowrie excelled allowed the shell money to have a lifespan that is only rivaled by a few other monies. Beginning with its early recordings in China around 3000 BCE, cowries retained monetary value and were legal currencies in parts of India and Africa until the eighteenth century. Only then, nearly 5,000 years later, did cowrie shells finally cease to be used as money.

To understand where different forms of money succeed and fail, one must always consider the three functions of money: unit of account, medium of exchange, and store of value. Money does not need to excel with all three properties to succeed, but to survive over time, it must always maintain the best combination of these three functions. Throughout history, people have always gravitated toward superior forms of money. Inferior money does not last.

YAP'S STONE MONEY

To demonstrate an example of a money that excelled specifically at one function, we can look to the islands of Yap. Yap, a group of ten small islands in the western Pacific Ocean, is known for its stone money, either known as Fei or Rai. Rai stones are large, round stones made of limestone. These stones vary wildly in size, ranging from diameters as small as an inch to as large as thirteen feet.[5]

Limestone is not native to the Yap islands. Instead, it was discovered on a nearby island named Palau. While there is some evidence that the Yapese first mined Palau limestone around 500 CE, it was not until between 1000 CE and 1400 CE that mining became more common. Once mined, the limestone was carved into large circular shapes, likely because a circular shape was easier to transport. A pole was put through the center of the Rai stones so groups of men could carry them, at which point they would be brought back to the Yap islands by boat. These stones quickly became valuable on the islands.

The reason that Rai stones became so valuable was due to their scarcity. With limestone not being available on the Yap islands, there was no way for most individuals to go out and acquire the limestone themselves. The limestone mining process was very primitive, so new Rai stones could not be created quickly or easily. The difficulty with mining limestone also meant that Rai stones were near impossible to counterfeit.

What developed from this is an exciting and unique system of trade. Large Rai stones, the largest of which weighed multiple tons, could not be carried or physically moved at all by a single person. When ownership of the stones was transferred from one person to another, the stone would typically stay in the same location as when it was in the possession of the previous owner. Rai stones were located all over the Yap islands, sitting in fixed spots, and ownership would transfer purely orally. This system worked quite well for the Yapese for hundreds of years. Due to the Rai stones' scarcity, the stones held value remarkably well throughout decades and even centuries.

It was not until the Europeans first descended on Yap's islands that the system of money based on Rai stones began to fail. After finding the islands, the Europeans introduced the Yapese to iron tools, which led to significant efficiencies in limestone mining and notably increased the amount of Rai stones that could be created. With Rai stones no longer as scarce as they once were, the currency underwent a period of high inflation beginning in the late nineteenth century, and the value of Rai stones dropped sharply.

It is worthwhile to examine precisely why the Rai stone succeeded for so many years. It was not easy to price all goods in Rai stones because the stones varied significantly in size. They could also not be physically transferred easily from person to person, meaning that you could not merely bring the stone into your home to claim possession. Instead, what allowed Rai stones such impressive longevity was how they excelled as stores of value. By being limited in supply due to the difficulty involved in mining and crafting the stones combined with the durability of limestone itself, Rai stones allowed the Yapese to use the currency to store wealth and maintain value over hundreds of years. Not many currencies can claim this feat.

MESOPOTAMIA—WHY MONEY BECAME METAL

O VER THE COURSE of thousands of years, systems of money gradually became more sophisticated. Through repeated trial and error—since most monies failed quickly—societies began to recognize specific characteristics that made for better money. At the same time, the development of agriculture progressed more rapidly. Communities were continually growing more and more food, and food security among many populations increased. This growth reached a turning point with the dawn of Mesopotamia.

Ancient Mesopotamia was a region located in the eastern Mediterranean, corresponding to much of modern-day Iraq and sections of Iran, Syria, and Turkey. Mesopotamia is essential to study because it is one of the first regions in human history where the people could produce enough food at a significant scale. This allowed members of the population to spend their days focused on tasks outside of food production.

Previously, in ancient communities, food was mostly all that mattered. While there were certain crafts on the side, the main job for any person—particularly men—was to procure food. In Mesopotamia, this was no longer the case. For the first time, many people could spend their days focused on other goals. This resulted in an incredible amount of human progress.

GREAT ADVANCEMENTS

NEARLY EVERY ASPECT of human knowledge was advanced by the Mesopotamians.

- Medicine
- Mathematics
- Science
- Astronomy
- Writing
- Religion
- Money

It is important to recognize that unlike the ancient civilizations of Egypt and Greece (both of which will be studied later in the following chapters), Mesopotamia was not unified by law. The region was instead more of a collection of varied cultures, social norms, and traditions. What unified the area was their common form of writing, religion, and the willingness to trade over long distances. Large-scale trade completed over great distances had never previously been conducted to the degree it was in Mesopotamia.

One area in which the Mesopotamians provided many advancements was within the field of language. Sumerian, one of the languages to develop during this time, is one of the oldest written languages in history.[6] It is believed that the Sumerian language came into being around 3100 BCE.

Many of the first things written in Sumerian were strictly related to business matters. Recording transactions and ledgers dominated early Sumerian writing. The Mesopotamians realized the importance of having a written log to track debts and inventory. This tracking allowed for a degree of sophistication within the economy to develop that was not possible before the invention of written ledgers.

The Mesopotamian region did not have an exceptionally diverse set of natural resources, though what it did have was used well. As such, the items used for money came either from the region or were acquired via trade. In the early development of civilization in the area, barley was one of the most common forms of commodity money typically used for trade.

After a while, a system involving clay tokens began to emerge. Clay tokens were crafted to represent goods, debts, and payments between people in the population. These pieces were one of the earliest forms of "symbolic money," meaning that the clay token represented ownership of a second different good.

At the onset, there were three commonly found types of clay tokens: one for grains, one for human labor, and one for livestock. Individuals crafted these marks by taking clay, molding them into one of the three shapes—often with distinct carvings—and baking them so that they hardened enough to withstand trade and circulation.

These tokens represented physical quantities of certain goods and were used to track the trades from one individual to another. They were not issued by any administering body, such as a government. Instead, they represented the trades and debts among individuals themselves. While the system began with three tokens, it eventually expanded to sixteen different pieces, all of which represented commonly traded goods. While it worked for a while, the system eventually became too unwieldy to function. There were simply too many tokens.

It bears repeating that the scope of the Mesopotamian economy far exceeded anything that had come before it.

No longer burdened by the constant need to produce more food, the Mesopotamians had more free time, and people used that time productively. While money had regularly developed in earlier societies, it was needed more than ever in Mesopotamia. With an economy operating at such scale, it was no longer good enough to use old and highly flawed forms of money. Mesopotamians drove humanity's progress forward in many technological fields. Alongside this progress, money had to evolve as well.

FROM CLAY TO SILVER

AT SOME POINT, less than a thousand years after the emergence of the clay tokens, silver began to emerge as the preferred medium of exchange for the region. Silver worked better than clay tokens for a variety of reasons. It was durable and could withstand circulation, it was portable, and the new supply of the metal was relatively consistent year to year. Silver was also already valued highly in Mesopotamia for decorative purposes.

Since silver was already prized and considered valuable in Mesopotamia, the amount of silver needed for transactions was quite small. As exchanging silver became more common, a formal standard of money was eventually needed. This led to the development of the "shekel."

The shekel marks a key point in the history of money. For the first time, a genuine form of money was named and designed specifically for its monetary properties. Goods and services became priced in shekels, made of silver. The shekel is a crucial distinction from earlier periods where commodity goods were money, but those goods were not explicitly used for monetary purposes.

Shekels were not coins, although they did function in

a similar role. There was no designated shape or size that constituted a shekel. Instead, shekels were determined by weight. Roughly a third of an ounce of silver equaled one shekel.

Shekels of silver were not a perfect form of money in Mesopotamia, however. Silver was always valuable in the region, and once it became a commonly accepted medium of exchange, it acquired an additional monetary premium. Since silver was valued so highly, many goods were priced in tiny quantities of silver. A pound of barley might cost only 3/100ths of a shekel.[7] This difficulty with small units led to a few different problems.

Using such small weights of silver for everyday purposes made it difficult to weigh and store. An ounce of silver has the same weight as a small, personal-sized bag of potato chips yet is much denser and takes up a smaller area. Three percent of a shekel could be as small as the size of your fingernail and almost as thin. It was challenging to get accurate measurements of such small weights. Since silver was so valuable, slight differences in these small measurements could result in a notable amount of lost monetary value.

In addition to the issues with measurement, counterfeit and fraud were also common when exchanging Mesopotamian silver. Since silver was incredibly valuable, there was an incentive for users of the money to try to pass off other metals as silver. Since the weights of silver exchanged were so tiny for many goods, it was difficult to detect counterfeit metals. Fraud was so common with early monies, not just in Mesopotamia, that the Old Testament of the Bible has numerous passages that explicitly forbid tampering with scales for exchange or substituting light stones for heavier ones.[8]

Many of the earliest forms of banking began during the

Mesopotamian era. Valuable items were stored in temples for safekeeping, similar to modern-day storage centers. Temples within Babylon, a capital city of the region, began to take on great wealth. Besides being used for storage, temples were regularly gifted donations that were then redistributed to people in need, often widows, orphaned children, or others.

After many decades—and even centuries—many temples had acquired massive amounts of wealth. Unsure of how exactly to use the money, the concept of banking in the way that we think of today began to form. Priests at the temples began to issue loans, both to the poor and to entrepreneurs looking to use the money for business. Often these loans were given to farmers. Thanks to the Mesopotamians' records, we can see that the earliest forms of the banking system still used today were started during this time. From this point forward, money and financial services increasingly became more sophisticated. Because of Mesopotamia, a new stage in the story of money had begun.

ANCIENT
EGYPT – GRAIN BANKS

C OMPARED TO MESOPOTAMIA, ancient Egypt had both a more and less sophisticated approach to money. Egypt operated under a form of feudalism. The structure of the society was hierarchical, similar to that of a pyramid. Above all were the gods, who the Egyptians believed could control the universe. They thought that the gods could control all aspects of society. If the Nile River overflooded, it was because the gods were angry. Below the gods, the Egyptians believed in order and class. There were strict delineations of people who resided in each class.

A TIGHTLY STRUCTURED SOCIETY

IN DESCENDING ORDER, Egyptian power followed a strict structure.

- Pharaohs
- Government Officials and Nobles
- Scribes
- Merchants
- Artisans
- Farmers
- Slaves and Servants

When a person was born into one class, it was unlikely that

they would ever move upwards or downwards in the hierarchical scheme. Social mobility was not encouraged whatsoever, and the lower classes did not often try. It was the belief that the gods had intended for the system to function this way to maintain order and keep as much peace among the people as possible.

This economy was also wholly centralized. The pharaoh was the owner of everything and the choice was up to him how to dole out goods. The pharaoh's top officials were not paid in currency for their work. Instead, they received what was necessary to live. Everything—food, clothing, shelter, land, etc.—was discretionary. This feudalistic system made it difficult for any form of societal currency to be established. Any good of actual value, such as gold or silver, was only accessible to the upper classes and not to the lowest ones. There was no clearly defined money for Egypt.

While people occasionally exchanged goods, there were not markets in the traditional sense, resulting in an economy that frequently involved barter. When trade occurred, the goods exchanged were often priced using one of a few units of account. The Egyptian economy was predominately based on the good that was most commonly grown in the area. This good was grain.

A SOPHISTICATED BANKING SYSTEM

WHEREAS THE ELITES held gold and silver, grain was much more commonly accessible to everyone. Grown by farmers in large quantities, grain became a widely used medium of exchange. Goods in Egyptian society often became priced in either gold, silver, or copper, but those metals were not used in trade. They functioned only as units of account, with grain becoming the most common good to exchange physically. This allowed for a system that did not entirely use traditional money but was also not quite barter either.

Since grain was so commonly grown and accepted for trade in Egypt, the question of storage began to arise. Ancient Egyptian governments centralized grain storage in large, state-run warehouses that allowed for security and convenience. Farmers, or any depositors, could safely store and withdraw grain whenever needed. There was a fee for people to store grain in the banks, used to pay state workers. As the system developed, depositors would receive a form of receipt for their deposit, which was occasionally used as a medium of exchange while trading. These grain banks eventually became quite large and worked in a sophisticated manner. It is reasonable to assert that the ancient Egyptian grain banks operated with a scale and complexity comparable to the modern banking system.

Compared to the Mesopotamians, ancient Egyptian society was less free and more structured. Due to the Egyptian economy's strict hierarchical structure, there was no opportunity for lower-class citizens to advance upward. The controlled nature of the economy meant that society operated with more primitive forms of money than developed in Mesopotamia. Since everything was controlled by the pharaoh and the officials carrying out his orders, there was significantly smaller direct-scale trade happening among the lower classes. What was needed or earned, such as food, was often given directly instead of workers earning money to buy what they chose.

Mesopotamia's economy was much less structured, and as a result, individuals had much more individual freedom. The Mesopotamian region had a considerably more sprawling economy with many more diffuse cultures spread throughout the region. Because of this, there was less cohesion with what the population used for money.

When comparing the two economies, one should note the trade-offs for each society. While the Egyptians were efficient with their closed-loop economy, the Mesopotamians are remembered for their numerous breakthroughs in writing, mathematics, science, and technology. Societal improvements were more limited in the Egyptian region than the Mesopotamian one. This limitation is why free societies tend to excel when compared to more tightly controlled ones. Innovation arises when individuals are allowed to use their creativity to solve problems.

While the Mesopotamian region can be seen gradually progressing alongside the forms of money being used throughout hundreds and thousands of years, eventually finding themselves organically operating in a silver-denominated economy, the Egyptians instead developed the sophistication of the institutions within their more primitive money system. Despite these differences, however, both regions would eventually find themselves using coins as the next primary phase in monetary history took place.

ANCIENT GREECE – THE DEVELOPMENT OF COINS

A ROUND 1000 BCE a monumental shift in the history of money occurred—the development of coins. Money was already progressing in this direction, with some societies using weights of metals as money, but the dawn of coins marked a new advancement with how money functioned. Unlike more primitive forms of money, the shape of coins could be standardized. Having a fixed size and weight allowed for more trust in the money, which allowed for more efficient trade.

Compared to earlier monies, coins represented a clear advancement in their ability to meet the properties of money. Coins were durable since they were made from metal and were portable since they were often small in size. No longer could grains of silver be diluted with lesser metals from a counterfeiter, as was the case in Mesopotamia. Coins represented an improvement in counterfeit resistance, though they were not foolproof. As coin technology grew more advanced, it became more challenging to counterfeit their design.

COINS IN THE BEGINNING

THE HISTORY OF coins begins in China. Research shows that cowrie shells were valued in China as early as the Shang

Dynasty, which ruled from approximately 1700 BCE to 1150 BCE.[9] The cowries frequently passed from high-ranking government officials and nobles to their lower-class subjects. Aside from cowries themselves, the Chinese later began making imitation bronze cowrie shells. These, too, had value.

Progressing from bronze cowries, the first proto-coins began being used. These took the form of small spades or knife-shaped objects made of metal, typically bronze. While they were not coins in the way often thought of today, functionally they were similar. These spade and knife-shaped coin-type items were immediately recognizable when used for trade and they were durable.

A common theme regarding early Chinese money is that the money often had a hole somewhere in its design. This hole allowed for the users of the money to string many of these early proto-coins together. This feature was significant since early Chinese money often favored less precious metals, such as bronze. Since bronze was more abundant than metals like silver and gold, a higher quantity of the metal was needed to conduct trade.

One of the first coins came from the city of Ephesus in ancient Lydia, which is now Turkey. Around 650 BCE, coins made from electrum—a natural alloy of silver and gold— were minted and were shaped similarly to a bean.[10] One side of the coin would have an official mark on it, such as an image of a lion. While electrum is a natural alloy and was found locally in the area, the government attempted to secure the stability of the coin's value by adding additional silver to the alloy while minting to ensure a 55% gold to 45% silver ratio.

In the middle of the sixth century, the Lydian King Croesus abandoned the electrum coins and created new coins made of pure gold and silver.[11] These coins, known as croeseids, are often considered the first truly standardized coins made from these precious metals. Gold and silver were valued to this point, but it was the standardization of heights, shapes, and weights that allowed the metals to flourish in the role of money.

While the first coins appeared in Lydia, ancient Greece was the first major economy to thrive under a system of coinage. Appearing in Greece around 600 BCE, the first coins in the region were made of silver and were stamped with an image of a turtle on one side, representing the country's history with trade by the sea. Political decisions did not drive the adoption of coins in Greece. Instead, it came from demand, convenience, and necessity. An ever-increasing number of mercenary soldiers demanded payment for their service, and it was beneficial for the state to adopt a form of money that everyone embraced.

The minting process for Greek coins was more advanced than anything that had come before. Metals were put in a large forge hearth where they were then melted. The molten metal was then poured into molds to keep the coins' size, shape, and weight standardized. At this point, an engraver was brought in to carve the needed design on one side of the coin.[12] Many attempts were made to counterfeit early coins by using a less valuable metal as a base with a thin layer of the correct metal as a coating. To counter this, the design of coins gradually became more complex.

The design of coins in Ancient Greece typically varied by city-state, known as a *"polis."* The typical organizational structure of a *polis* consisted of a sacred center built on an acropolis or the water, a fortified urban center, and additional land surrounding the city center. It was prevalent to use gods from Greek mythology as the design for coins, but designs were not limited to these figures. The most well-known design of ancient Greek coins is the owl of Athena, which appeared on the tetradrachm coins in Athens.

IMPROVING ECONOMIC EFFICIENCY

THE ECONOMY OF ancient Greece relied predominantly on trade with other regions. Greece had poor soil for farming and was only able to grow a limited group of vegetables and other plant goods. Still, agriculture was the foundation of the Greek economy, with nearly 80% of the population taking part in agricultural production.[13] The vast majority of what was grown, and therefore eaten by the Greek people, was barley. While there is evidence that the ancient Greeks believed that wheat was a more nutritious grain than barley, barley was a less demanding crop to grow, producing more crop in less space.

Barley and olives were the two core crops that were produced in ancient Greek society. The rocky land and difficult soil of the region were well suited for the growth of olive trees. Growing olives is a long-term investment. The trees take twenty years to grow and only provide olives for harvest every other year. To round out the standard diet, these crops were supplemented by other vegetables such as beans, cabbage, chickpeas, garlic, lentils, and onions. Almond, apple, fig, and pear trees were also grown.[14]

Trade was a fundamental part of how the Greek economy functioned. Much of this trade was conducted via maritime commerce, where goods were bought from and sold to countries along the Mediterranean Sea. A trade network developed between Greece, Egypt, Asia Minor—an area near modern-day Turkey which included Lydia—and small islands such as Crete and Cyprus.[15] The evolution towards coinage in Greece coincided with the development of specialized ships for merchants around 600 BCE, which resulted in even more efficient maritime trade. Merchants from many different nationalities would meet at permanently established trading posts where all sorts of goods were exchanged.

It is no coincidence that the advancement of Greek technology and efficiency, such as the construction of higher-quality ships, occurred once the Greeks began to adopt coins as money. Having a reliable and consistent base layer of money allows for significantly improved economic efficiency. When inferior currencies are used, people in a population often have to spend much of their time preserving their individual wealth. This is the distinct differentiator between goods that function well as money and those that do not—the ability to store wealth over time.

When a nation's economy uses a form of money with superior wealth-keeping properties, such as silver coins, it gives those using the currency the security that the currency will maintain value. The ability to store wealth is a form of economic freedom, as it allows the masses to focus squarely on their businesses. When people do not have to worry that their currency will quickly lose value, they can take a long-term approach to life through the ability to plan for the future, instead of being stuck focusing on day-to-day survival as bad money necessitates.

It is with ancient Greece that there begins to be a clear delineation between the primitive economies before it and the more modern economies that followed. The predominant form of economic activity in Greece was still agriculture but commerce was undeniably crucial in Greek society.

It was not until about 500 BCE that there began to be the beginnings of a significant industrial revolution in Greece, fueled by the continued adoption of coinage. In the largest *poleis,* such as Athens and Corinth, there began to be areas of specialization and technological improvements. During this period, the Greeks developed iron tools that were so advanced they were later used both by the Romans and in Ptolemaic Egypt.[16] Prosperity became more widespread since workers were finally able to store their newfound wealth over time. Before coinage, this was not possible. The development of coins led to a natural decline in aristocratic patronage and the rise of a more market-based economy and democratically governed Greece.

The banking system in Greece was quite developed as well. Interestingly, banks in ancient Greece operated under a full-reserve banking system, meaning that 100% of a client's deposits were kept in reserve at the bank. Banks were not used as sources of credit, nor was interest on deposits allowed. Instead, banks functioned as money warehouses of sorts. They were explicitly designed so that a depositor would feel secure knowing that their money would always be there if they wanted to withdraw it. The banking system was based solely on trust; there were no legal guarantees protecting deposits. Trustworthy institutions gained reputation through accountability, word of mouth, and reliability with servicing withdrawals.

As money continued to develop throughout history, so did the sophistication and scale of the largest communities, nations, and regions. These two progressions are closely related. One of the benefits of money is that it allows us to store time itself. If a worker earns a wage for one day's work, that worker has essentially converted their time into money. When money loses its value over time, it is equivalent to time having been wasted or stolen. For example, imagine that the wage the worker earned for their day of work loses half of its purchasing power within a month. If the worker did not spend their money immediately, that worker essentially worked for a full day but is left with only a half day's purchasing power a month later, because of the devaluation of the money.

Poor forms of money are incapable of holding their value over time, which is the great downfall of so many currencies both in ancient times and today. Before coins became popular, there were very few forms of money that held value well. Coins represented the first time that a valuable form of money could be easily standardized while allowing the users of the money to store their wealth more efficiently than ever before. This ability to save gave workers of all classes a level of security with their finances. Instead of continuously worrying about their wealth and needing to spend their money immediately, coins allowed workers to store some of their wealth over time.

Alongside the growth of coins came the advancement of many great nations, regions, and empires. This growth would not have been possible without the continued improvement in how money developed. This can be seen further with the dawn of ancient Rome.

ROME – THE RISE AND FALL

F OLLOWING THE ADVANCEMENT of Greece were the
beginnings of the Roman Empire. While the two societies grew at roughly the same point in history, the Romans
did not ascend into a dominant power until sometime after
300 BCE, where the advances in money by the Greeks
occurred before that point.

ROME'S BEGINNINGS

LEGEND HAS IT that Rome was founded by twin brothers,
Romulus and Remus, who were the sons of the god Mars.
The legend states that during an argument over who would
rule the city, Romulus killed Remus. Romulus named the
city after himself, and thus Rome was born.[17]

The true beginnings of ancient Rome were likely much
timider. Beginning as a small town around the eighth century BCE, Rome was located on the banks of the Tiber
River. Through trade, the population grew in size and managed to become a hub for economic activity.

To the north of early Rome was Etruria, a region that
includes modern-day Tuscany. Already a developed metrop-
olis, Etruria and the Etruscans provided a blueprint for how
to conduct trade and were an important influence on
Rome's development in the earliest stages of its growth.
Rome's expansion from a small town to a city of considerable

size was rapid due to the Romans' penchant for taking the trade skills they had learned from other regions and improving those methods to further spur efficiency.

Over the period from 800 BCE to 600 BCE, Rome became a proper city whose territory was ruled by a king. The seventh and final king of Rome, Lucius Tarquinius Superbus, was detested by the people. He was infamous for his use of violence as a method of control and his disrespect for Roman customs and the Roman Senate. The backlash against the king was so significant that it inspired a revolution. The king was overthrown in 509 BCE and the period of monarchy ended in Rome. Rome shifted to a more democratic style of governance and became a republic.

As much as ancient Rome conjures mental images of grandeur, its economy was not particularly complex when compared with modern economies. It was a slave-based economy based heavily on agriculture due to the large population of the ever-growing region. There was some industrial production as well, but this paled in comparison to the size of its agricultural and trade businesses.

In the early days of the Roman Republic, coins had not yet made their way to the region. Instead, the Romans used weights of bronze as their medium of exchange. The measurements in bronze, known as the *"aes rude,"* were quite large, with one unit of money being the equivalent of 11.5 oz (324 g) in weight.[18] While this was a cumbersome way to price goods, fractional units were used as well. Eventually, this developed into the beginnings of coinage in the Roman Republic.

The first Roman coins were minted in the late fourth century BCE and were also made of bronze. As with other regions, Roman coins represented a significant evolution in the progression of their economy. Coins were widely recognized as valuable and were easily identifiable and guaranteed to be accepted by merchants, allowing for the easy transfer of value. This in turn allowed for easier commerce and storage of wealth, raising the quality of life for all users of the money.

Bronze is not a particularly good metal to be money, however. The choice of which metal to use for money had a significant impact on an economy. While coins, even when made out of copper or bronze, represented an upgrade in scarcity compared to earlier millennia, these metals were still relatively abundant. The ease at which new metal could be found and turned into coinage reduced the wealth storing ability of metals like copper and bronze since the currency supply could be diluted relatively easily.

THE IMPACT OF WAR

AT THE TIME of the Second Punic War, which occurred around 218 BCE-201 BCE, the Romans' bronze monetary standards began to fall apart. While bronze can work as money in some circumstances, it requires the civilization using bronze to have limited access to the metal to preserve its scarcity. Rome was not strictly limited in this regard. Having already grown to a power of considerable size, the Roman government had acquired significant stores of copper—the primary metal in the alloy bronze—to mint as currency. When war arose, it became prudent for new coins to be minted to fund the continuing battles, leading to a flooding of the market for bronze coins, which then lost their value.

War is among the most common reasons a currency collapses. Under the premise of the necessity of the war, a nation will do whatever it can to win. For battles that rage on for many years, it frequently becomes difficult to pay for the ongoing fight. Soldiers need food, supplies, and weapons. War is simply expensive. Since most governing states believe that it is necessary that they not only fight the battles they fight but also that they win them, the *modus operandi* eventually becomes to pay for war at all costs.

Even in ancient times, governments and kings were limited in raising money to fund wars. Operationally, there are only two options: collect a tax or increase the supply of the money. When it comes to the scale of war, collecting a tax to pay for the proceedings is neither wise nor feasible. War is often too expensive to be paid for by tax revenues. This cost inevitably leads to an influx of new currency, minted by the ruling class, to fund the war.

While this may work temporarily—long enough for a war to be won—it often has destructive effects on the currency in the longer term. A money does not succeed through its scarcity in the absolute, meaning how much of the metal, or whatever is being used for currency, is in places such as the earth's crust or inaccessible areas across the globe. The scarcity of a money instead has to do with how rare it is to that currency's users.

Bronze can work well in a society that has no means to mine or acquire any more bronze. Bronze does not work well, however, when bronze is easy to acquire and the scarcity of the currency is determined solely by the discipline of the minting body. When war breaks out, discipline goes out the window. The supply of the currency greatly expands and the money loses value. This loss of value leads to a downward spiral and eventual currency collapse.

At this point, Roman currency shifted toward silver as the predominant monetary base metal. Silver coins had already been minted in Rome for a while, they were just used less frequently than bronze coins. As Rome had continued to grow in size and trading stature over the previous centuries, the city continuously expanded the degree to which it traded with other regions. Much of this trade involved the Greeks. The Greeks had been using silver coins for several centuries prior to the Romans and thus, their economy was based on silver. Trading with the Greeks required becoming more compliant with their philosophy on money to most easily facilitate trade. This encouraged the use of silver.

While the Romans had a few silver coins circulating, it was the denarius that would become the dominant coin of the Roman economy. The denarius was first struck in 211 BCE and was the Roman economy's backbone for over five centuries.[19] The switch to silver allowed the Roman economy to thrive. The Romans had already contributed numerous advancements in modern language, politics, and government. Still, using the denarius, Rome saw itself emerge as a true world power. Innovations in warfare, architecture, and engineering all occurred, including contributions to society that are still used today.

By 51 BCE, Julius Caesar had conquered the region of Celtic Gaul, which was the first time Rome's borders spread outside of the Mediterranean.[20] While it still operated as a republican government, the power of Rome had begun to weaken. Julius Caesar was assassinated in 44 BCE and was replaced by his heir, Gaius Julius Caesar Octavianus. Shortly after that, Rome conquered Egypt. Octavian was granted lifelong power by the Senate, at which point he became the first Emperor of Rome.

Over the next 200 years, the Roman economy continued to grow and thrive. By 200 CE, however, growth began to slow, and the ruling class's attempts to stimulate the economy proved to do more harm than good.

THE DEVALUATION OF THE DENARIUS

THERE ARE A few reasons for the slowing of economic growth around this time. After two centuries of continued expansion, in which an advanced road network was created that allowed trade all over the region, the Romans started running out of areas to conquer. The lack of new territory meant that they could no longer seize new revenue streams from the new settlements they had annexed, which they had done throughout Rome's expansion.

There is no better representation for the fall of the Roman economy than by understanding the devaluation of the denarius. At its original minting, the denarius weighed 4.5 grams of 100% silver.[21] It stayed this way for a few hundred years, but eventually, the Roman rulers could not resist the urge to devalue the coin. During the first century CE, the denarius maintained a value of over 90% silver. By the end of the second century, however, the coin's silver content had fallen to less than 70% purity. From this point on, the devaluation was already on an irreversible course, and by 300 CE there was less than 5% silver in the coin.

If Rome's rulers knew that their devaluation of the denarius would lead to economic collapse, why would they devalue the coin in the first place? Alas, this is a frequent occurrence throughout history, and inflation is undoubtedly the most common natural cause of currency collapse. Often, a growing economy reaches a point where the promised expenditures surpass what can be collected in tax revenue. This deficit happens through the natural economic debt cycles that every economy goes through as long as debt and credit are accessible.

As an economy grows, the amount of debt in the economy grows as well. When an economy is booming, this is fine because incomes and wealth are increasing alongside the debt, so the owed burden is not becoming larger relative to income. The growth in an economy leads to increased economic confidence by the people, which increases the amount of debt further, as there is high confidence in continued growth. Eventually, however, debt growth outpaces income growth. When this happens, those who owe money begin to feel the burdens they have committed to more acutely.

While there are many reasons for the fall of the Roman Empire, it is necessary to understand the monetary role in its decline. As Rome grew and expanded its scope and power, its military necessarily grew as a result. War is expensive, and the Romans engaged in constant warfare to conquer new territory and expand Rome's control into new areas. There was an ever-increasing need for more soldiers—more soldiers, more weapons, and more battles. These soldiers required pay for their work. Additionally, many of the soldiers were mercenaries, meaning they had no loyalty to Rome other than the prospect of getting rewarded with monetary compensation for their time.

As Rome—and its military—grew, it became increasingly difficult for the Roman government to afford its military's rising costs. It was not just the military that had this problem. Besides the military, the power of the Roman government and the church greatly expanded alongside the rise of the Roman Empire. All three institutions had significant levels of corruption, which made it more challenging to allocate capital efficiently. The military was the most significant factor, however. Soldiers were the conquerors of new territory and they were relied upon to protect the ever-expanding borders of Rome. It was of the utmost importance to the Roman government that the military remained mighty.

It was not just prioritizing the strength of the military that was essential to those who ruled Rome. It is often difficult to roll back programs that have already begun, meaning that it is common for government institutions to grow in size and power over time gradually. This dynamic often mimics the happenings of economic cycles. As Rome grew, the size of the government, including the military, grew with it. At a certain point, costs began to rise faster than revenues did, making it necessary to decide between two responsible choices: either decrease spending or increase taxes. Of course, politicians often do not choose between the two prudent decisions. Instead, they devalue the currency.

Politically, devaluing the currency is the easiest choice and one that is commonly made. Decreasing spending is the least politically palpable for numerous reasons. Primarily, once a system is established that benefits people, users of that system become dependent on its existence. When the costs of running that system, a government program, or the military become too high, it is not easy to simply cancel the institution. Users of a government service shift how they go through their daily lives, knowing that they can rely on the service to perform its intended goal. If that reliability goes away, it harms people more than if the program had never been established in the first place. Due to how this works, once a government has expanded, it rarely shrinks later on. By the decline of the Roman Empire, Rome had covered an enormous area and its central government was of great size. As it grew, costs eventually outpaced growth.

As such, political pressures and rising costs made it impossible to pay what was owed in full. Instead, as mentioned above, the minters of the denarius chose to attempt to inflate away the rising costs through the devaluation of the currency. In essence, this is theft through manipulated depreciation. Soldiers and others were promised a certain amount of denarius coins, but since the ruling class could not afford the payments, they lessened the value of the currency itself.

As mentioned earlier in this chapter, the depreciation of the denarius coincided with the Roman Empire's fall. This is not a coincidence. Instead, the two are inextricably linked. When a civilization or an empire believes that it has no choice other than to devalue its currency, that nation is often already in the midst of an irreversible decline.

Rome ruled for many centuries. Numerous aspects of modern human life developed, improved, or were innovated during the time of the Rome's dominance. The Roman Empire permanently altered the development of the human species for the better. Analyzing the rise and the fall, however, shows the importance of a currency in a civilization's success. Reliable money allows for growth and security. When the reliability of the currency is tampered with, typically for political reasons, the civilization's dominance eventually falls.

CELTIC COINS—EARLY ENGLISH MONEY

As the history of money heads towards the medieval period and the development of the British pound, it is worth first examining the contributions of early Celtic coinage. Because the rise of Rome often overshadows the period of Celtic tribes, the Celtic approach to coinage is overlooked.

THE EFFECT OF ROME'S FALL IN BRITAIN

Celtic tribes were scattered across northwestern Europe. Their first coins, appearing around 200 BCE, were coins that were indigenous to the Celtic peoples. This area was then later conquered by Rome, and thus Roman coinage began to dominate the region. Roman coins, particularly the silver denarius, were superior to the coins that Celtic tribes used. Still, Celtic coins continued to be used in particularly distant regions.

After the fall of the Roman Empire, there were 300 to 400 years where there was no strong currency. This period, and many centuries after it, is collectively known as the Dark Ages in Europe. This designation is understandable when considering the immense power that Rome held. Not only was Rome powerful, but it ruled a vast amount of territory. When Rome fell and was no longer able to control all of these territories, a power vacuum formed. Regions that had become reliant on Rome's centralized power had to come up with new methods of governance and, importantly, new currencies for the areas.

Currencies began to pop up in various areas, but they were often poorly considered. When Rome fell, many regions understood that coins were the best form of money to date, but they did not correctly account for the difficulties that arise with a new coin's minting. Early coins were typically short-lived before they would collapse. After the region of England had no consistent form of money for a few centuries, the earliest form of the English penny developed.

The first Celtic coins found in early Britain were made of gold. These coins were close imitations of nearby Macedonian coins, but as the Celtic confidence with coin minting grew, the designs in which they minted became gradually more complex. For example, horses were a highly valued animal in Celtic culture, so having a horse on the design was a strongly favored design.[22] At this point, other metals such as silver and bronze began to be used as coinage as well.

When the Romans came to conquer Britain during their rule, they found a country of Celtic-language-speaking people. This did not notably change throughout Roman reign. By the time the Romans left the region, a bit after 400 CE, Britain was still a Celtic land. While the Roman languages did make some headway in the area, other aspects of Roman culture, such as the Christian religion, did not affect many Celtic natives. The culture itself may not have translated to the Celtic people, but the fact that there was a modern economy did help the region. Romans integrated with and developed the areas, bringing relative economic prosperity to the region.

Because of this, the fall of the Roman Empire was a significant step back for the area in terms of societal sophistication. This was true in many places, but Britain faced particularly harsh extremes from this reality. In a manner of decades, what was once a relatively modern economy devolved into a system of money with hastily crafted coins and proto-barter among disjointed and disrupted markets. Britain reverted to a much more primitive economy, and the quality of life for the people decreased significantly. There is a special meaning to this period of the Dark Ages in Britain. As the Roman influence disappeared, the region faced difficult times.

It was not until the sixth or seventh century that new forms of coinage made their way back to parts of Western Europe. Much like before, these coins were not created within the area but were instead brought there by travelers. These coins were originally made of gold, but it was not long before the gold was alloyed with silver and eventually replaced entirely by silver. This is important to note for coins in Britain from this point forward were almost always entirely silver. The reason for this was scarcity.

While the point has been made many times thus far that scarcity is an essential property in the longevity of a currency—a factor that has allowed gold to remain valuable for 5,000 years—a money can be too scarce to properly function. Suppose there is not enough money in an economy. In that case, the money will not be used as a generally accepted medium of exchange since not enough people will have access to the currency. Gold was not too scarce in the absolute, meaning that certain societies thrived using a system of gold, but it was too scarce for England. There was not enough gold in the country to be the standard metal for money. Thus, silver became the dominant metal used in Britain, which remained the case for over a millennium.

In fact, this was true of much of the world. When looking

back at the development of money from its first creation to the modern age, silver, not gold, has been the most commonly used money throughout history. Silver was the better metal for many societies. It was not nearly as abundant as highly available metals such as bronze or copper, yet it was also not as scarce as gold, which allowed it to function well as both a medium of exchange and a store of value for many societies. As we will see later, as trade became increasingly global and gold became more widely available, the economic strength of countries using gold-based currencies consistently surpassed countries based on silver.

By the eighth century, coins in Anglo-Saxon England were almost entirely silver, although they were sometimes alloyed with other metals such as bronze or copper. However, the area was still decidedly disjointed, with various rulers in control of different regions, all of whom were minting their own coins. Minters of coins with higher compositions of inferior metal could not compete with superior coins and those regions experienced increased economic hardship. It was not until 765 that a penny of good quality silver began to establish itself throughout England.

At this time, there was upheaval in the political structure of England. While there were seven traditional kingdoms of England, these kingdoms had become merged as one under the rule of the kings of Northumbria in the north and Mercia in the south. As the separate domains began to operate under a uniform control, so too would the forms of coinage begin to be standardized. Under this rule began a more uniform system of money, with engravings of the heads of kings becoming commonplace on coins again.

It was under the reign of Offa, who ruled from 757 to 796, that coinage in England truly began to find its footing. Like many currencies at the time, the English penny was modeled on another coin, known as the "denier" in Paris. Compared to most of the continental counterparts who followed the French's lead with the denier, the English version far surpassed the others in quality. The factor that allowed the English penny to become the dominant, however, was minting. Through the conquest and establishment of more minters, Offa was able to increase the production of high-quality English pennies to such a degree that their popularity began to spread over the entire continent of Europe. This marks the birth of English monetary dominance.

THE VIKING INFLUENCE

IT MUST BE mentioned that it was not only Offa and England that were contributing to the progression of monetary development at this time. It would be remiss to ignore the contributions of the Vikings. There is a reason that more English coins have been found in Scandinavia than in England. That reason is the raids by the Vikings. These raids began to happen around 790 CE. At first, the attacks were small, focused on pillaging and looting, but slowly became more akin to conquering outright. Eventually, the Vikings would not only take over foreign lands, but they would also remain there, permanently settled.

This was happening right as England had recently become unified among its seven kingdoms. The Vikings threw much of that unification into chaos. The settlement of the Vikings became such that much of northern England was controlled by the Vikings, which maintained an uneasy relationship with the nervous, native people of southern England.

This was a time of much back and forth and a lack of continuity regarding governance in England. There were repeated battles with the Vikings, attempts at a reunified England—although there was always fighting—and other difficulties perpetually arising. However, one key activity that remained constant was the increase in new mints for coins. Instead of devaluing the English currencies by reducing the amount of precious metal within each coin, the English prioritized creating more—and purer—coins.

While the production of new coins itself does lower the value of the currency by reducing its scarcity, the negative aspects of this are mitigated in a society where there is not already widespread access to money. While new silver coins were being produced, usage of those coins was spread throughout a sparsely populated island (by today's standards). Thus, the metal was still reliably scarce enough to function as quality money.

A NATIONAL CURRENCY ESTABLISHED

IN 928 CE, the Statute of Greatley was declared, which specified the need for a national currency. This would be the first time since Rome that there would be one currency to represent the region. However, this is easier said than done, and it took over one hundred years for this declaration to be established in practice. Even so, the declaration was quite significant. France would not achieve a national currency for more than another 600 years and Italy for nearly 900 years. This fact may surprise many readers. Indeed, this is the slow reality of monetary progression.

As a species, humans have engaged in primitive forms of trade for nearly our entire existence. The tendency is to think that our modern systems are a natural, gradual evolution where we consistently advanced. While accurate in some instances, monetary systems are much more nonlinear because money is not a single technological advancement. It is not akin to the development of the wheel or to electricity, where once it has been invented or discovered, it can now be available to all to advance a society. A system of money is much more delicate and can fail once it has been established.

First, there must be a natural progression for any society towards a good or metal that reasonably meets the properties of money, particularly scarcity. This priority can get ignored when a ruler promotes an inferior form of currency for adoption as the law of the land. Even if the correct commodity is chosen to be the money itself, management of that currency has led countless monies to fail. It is not common then, for a coin to become widely used among a large population, let alone for it to be adopted by an entire country. By coalescing around a natural currency so much earlier than many of its geographical neighbors, the region of Britain gained a massive economic advantage over its competitors, which it would leverage into becoming a global power over the next 1,000 years.

ISLAM – THE GOLDEN AGE

A DVANCEMENTS IN MONEY and economics were occurring elsewhere as well. By this point in history, coins were becoming used throughout Eurasia. Coins rapidly replaced inferior forms of money once they were introduced into local economies. This dissemination took time though, particularly in the ancient, pre-globalized world. Even beyond the slow speed at which coinage use spread, not all societies magically knew to use gold and silver for their coins. Instead, the growth of coinage was a game of trial and error with different metals, except with much more significant consequences.

When a currency fails, the quality of life for the users of that currency falls significantly because the financial system's economic production and efficiency cannot remain where it was without a reliable system of accounting—aka money. This difficulty led to many trials and almost as much error.

In the East, the Islamic Golden Age is typically dated to have begun near the eighth century. The period is known as a time when Islam started to flourish and became increasingly popular. Simultaneously, a level of economic prosperity came to be that had not previously occurred in the region. This relative prosperity was not limited in scope either. The area mentioned when talking about the Islamic Golden Age was vast, ranging from northern Africa, up into today's Middle East through Persia, and down towards

India. There were numerous advancements in art, science, economic development, and other cultural works during this period. The unifier—the common factor in the success of the area—was the money.

Prior to the beginnings of the Islamic Golden Age, there was much less standardized sophistication regarding money in the region. Since the early state of Islam was nowhere near its later size, there was neither the authority nor the opportunity to launch a new coin. Instead, a variety of coins were accepted from various other regions, such as Rome and Persia. Around 695, during the reign of the Umayyads, the first Arabic coins were minted. The dinar was minted in gold and the dirham was made of silver.[23]

THE FLOURISHING OF ISLAM

THE MINTING OF these first Arabic coins allowed for economic and political growth in many ways for the Umayyads. The establishment of a currency brings legitimacy and sovereignty to a new state, which no longer has to rely on the free form of circulating coins entering its borders. As many kings, governments, and tyrants have learned throughout the years, control over money means absolute power. The unification of the Islamic monetary standard allowed for greater and easier tax collection and allowed for the development of a more fully realized banking system. Alongside the growth of banking came the spread of other unique and innovative financial instruments, including a system of invoicing to request payments and a bill of exchange that allowed for the transfer of debt between parties.

As the supply of modern (for the time) Arabic coins began to grow exponentially, so too did the region's population. As has already been seen in various chapters throughout *The Story of Money*, this is likely no coincidence. The role money plays in the development of society extends far beyond the simple reach of traders. Money production increased and urbanization followed suit. A consistent form of money allowed for more accessible and more efficient trade, and as a result, people begin to settle in common locations—cities. Following the dinar and the dirham's adoption, urbanization in the Islamic region proliferated as more people herded to established areas to settle down and conduct trade.

Because of this, a period of intensive economic growth began. There was a significant expansion in irrigation, which led to substantial improvements in agricultural productivity. The manufacturing industry also grew as a result of urbanization. Both industries contributed to the development of trade conducted over longer distances and resulted in an average level of economic prosperity that was far above the minimum needed to survive.[24] This is the importance of money.

It is not just that money allows for more efficient exchange, though this is true. The major breakthrough that money allows is the ability to store wealth into the future. Not only has the productivity of the worker increased to where now they earn more from a day's work than is needed to survive, but now that worker can keep that extra wealth reserved for the future through a money that excels as a store of value.

Part of the reason that the dinar, weighing 4.25 grams of gold, became such an important coin was that it was used across a wide area of land. From parts of northeastern Africa to modern Iraq and even India, the dinar became an accepted currency. There were local flavors to the dinar, meaning different designs and mints, though the dinar always remained the same weight in gold, since one king did not control this region. Instead, what unified the region was the adoption of Islamic principles and compatible cultural beliefs.

A key development that allowed for Islamic culture to spread throughout the area was the discovery that the Chinese were making paper during this time period.[25] By importing Chinese paper and learning to make it themselves, it became much easier to transfer the written word. This led to the further development of scripture throughout the Islamic region. On the financial side, this allowed for the creation of a primitive version of checks.

The result of this was a highly functioning economy with significant trade and advancements in religion and culture in the region. The dinar was a strong backbone for an economy such as this, and the dual-metal system of gold and silver allowed users of the currencies to trade and store wealth with ease. Unfortunately, the golden age for Islam was nearing its end.

THE GOLDEN AGE ENDS

IN 1258, BAGHDAD was invaded by the Mongolians.[26] The attackers managed to destroy countless writings, manuscripts, and other religious institutions. The famous libraries that had grown during the expansion of Muslim culture were destroyed. The Islamic regions faced many more attacks around this time, from multiple different regions. The region was also invaded and attacked due to the crusaders' campaigns from the west. This combination of attacks fundamentally halted the area's progress, marking the Islamic Golden Age's unofficial end.

The many regions that progressed together during the

Islamic Golden Age broke away from each other, forming individual states that did not always get along. As there was much damage from the many battles that were fought, societal infrastructure had mostly fallen apart, leading to lowered living standards for a long time.

The dinar was still used, but it was not an effective money, as it had once been. Competing monies were brought into use as rulers of many of these newly established nations desired to have their own currency to control. This attempt at control was less efficient than during the golden age, where there were less rigidly structured states with fewer outright rulers in the region. As has been seen many times before, attempting to control a money often leads to worse outcomes for the people.

CHINA – PAPER MONEY

M OST OF US think that the development of money throughout history was linear, with a steady progression from where we started to where we are today. Thinking about money this way, however, can be misleading. The world is vast, and communication was limited between different regions until just recently. While a society, the Mesopotamians for example, may have stumbled into understanding the value of silver, that realization may not have reached other parts of the world for hundreds, if not thousands, of years.

Paper money was not invented by the Bank of England. Paper money is older than many may realize, and it presents a cautionary tale for all who do not question the structure of modern money today.

PRIVATELY ISSUED REDEEMABLE CERTIFICATES

THE FIRST PAPER money originated in China in the seventh century during the Tang dynasty, approximately 900 years before paper money usage in England.[27] Paper money became possible once the ability to print became available. While the proper printing press was not invented until the 1400s, the Chinese had developed a method for printing nearly 600 years earlier.

This early paper money, nicknamed "flying cash," due to its tendency to accidentally blow away in the wind, was essentially a certificate from the Tang government that guaranteed a certain amount of a good, such as metal or silk. The certificate was redeemable, meaning that it could be exchanged for the actual good it represented, but it was rare for this to be done. These certificates were not widely used. Their primary purpose was to pay merchants located far away from the region where the Tang lived, since metal would be difficult to transport over such large distances.

While the idea of paper certificates being used in a monetary sense occurred during the Tang dynasty, it was not until the Song dynasty, beginning in 960, that paper money began to emerge in a manner more akin to what is used today. In the province of Szechuan, where Chinese printing was first invented, upper-class merchants and banks conspired to create a form of banknote money. These first banknotes were quite extravagant in design, with pictures of trees, people, and homes printed on the notes with a flourish using red and black ink.

GOVERNMENT INVOLVEMENT

IN SZECHUAN, PAPER money began to become widely accepted quickly. The Chinese were early to adopt paper notes as money and credit had long been familiar concepts within Chinese culture. By 1024, the Chinese government had noticed the success of paper money in Szechuan and was not content to sit idly by as paper money was being issued through entirely private sources. The government made it law that only they could issue paper notes as money.

The notes created by the Chinese authorities were valued and redeemable for metal and were exchanged among people and merchants in regular trade. The banknotes could also be brought to government-owned shops to be directly exchanged for salt or liquor, which differed from later paper monies. The Chinese banknotes were directly redeemable for other goods and metals alike.

Paper money was used in China when Marco Polo first came to the region in the thirteenth century. Polo was quickly fascinated by the monetary system, to the point that he detailed it in his journals quite extensively.[28] He noted all aspects of the monetary system, including how money was produced, how it was valued, and the ways in which it was exchanged. Though not definitively proven, there is speculation that Polo's excitement about Chinese money upon his return is what sparked the idea of paper money in Europeans and contributed to its development there.

In the thirteenth century, the Mongols conquered China and established the Yuan dynasty, and changes to the monetary system happened swiftly. The Mongols were well coordinated and created a national money system that was not backed by either gold or silver. This monetary system is known as a "fiat" money system, which the entire world uses today. Fiat money has no value in itself, it is only valuable by decree. By carefully controlling the supply of the paper money to be relatively limited, the idea behind a fiat currency is that it allows the issuing body—the minter—of the money more direct control over the currency itself, which theoretically allows for a more stable economy.

It is a question that still gets asked today—why is paper money (or dollars) valuable? Answers to this question almost always overlook the five properties of money: divisibility, durability, portability, recognizability, and scarcity. A common refrain today is that dollars are backed by the trust in the American government or the strength in the military, but neither of these are strictly true. Money either works well or does not based on how it performs regarding money's five properties. While the paper itself may be relatively worthless, if a paper money is scarce, divisible, and counterfeit resistant, it truly functions well as money and deserves value.

It is the scarcity aspect where paper money tends to fail, and such was the case with the Mongols. It has proven to be impossible for an issuer of a money that has no limit, other than responsibility, to refrain from a devaluation of the currency. For the few hundred years throughout the Yuan and later Ming dynasties, inflation was a constant problem and there were numerous revaluations of the currency. Eventually, in 1450, the paper money experiment had failed so badly in China that they reverted to a metal-based system and ceased using paper.

THE DARK AGES–MEDIEVAL MONEY

A S SILVER MONEY continued to be minted in England, problems with quality began to arise. There were many mints throughout the region, with them all producing different qualities of coinage. The condition of coins deteriorated over the 200 or so years following the Statute of Greatley as more minters began to form. Minting coins was a lucrative and desirable business, but it was impossible to standardize the quality of the work that came from this many minters.

Coins were easily clipped, meaning that the coin's silver content was not always its required amount. Additionally, coins were so frequently counterfeit that it became customary to make a small slice in the coinage to see that the inside was pure silver instead of just silver-plated.

After the civil war that occurred in the mid-1100s, the currency's quality fell even further, to the point that it became a necessity to repair following the war. This responsibility fell to King Henry II, who managed to restore the excellence and prestige of English currency with the eventual development of the pound sterling.

The term "pound" was used before the re-branding of currency to being sterling. A pound referred to a weight of silver. Two hundred forty silver pennies were equal to one pound of silver. As part of King Henry II's re-imagining of the coin, English currency transitioned from pure 100% silver to an alloy of 90% silver.

Using an alloy allowed the currency to be physically harder, which is ideal for circulation. When a coin uses a softer metal, like gold and silver in their pure forms, the currency will get bent, deformed, and dented through the natural rigors of circulation. When alloyed with another metal, the coins become much stronger. The pound still represented a weight, however. There were no sterling pound coins. Instead, the coins that were used were pence and shillings. Twelve pence equaled one shilling, and twenty shillings equaled one sterling pound.

GOVERNING STRUCTURE

UP THROUGH THIS period, England operated under a feudal system not dissimilar to the governance style of the Egyptians. In England, the king was at the absolute top of the hierarchy, who was the sole owner of all of the country's land. Underneath the king were all other nobles, known as "vassals," who occupied the land in the name of the king. Besides the king, the nobles were considered near royalty and wielded tremendous power in the country.

This system necessarily dictates a top-down level of control over the population. Different groups among the hierarchical pyramid all occupied different social statuses and wielded progressively more power the closer they were to the king. To hold land at all—also known as being granted a "fief"—a person must be given the status of a vassal, which was done through a formal ceremony.

It was King Henry II who continued to reform various aspects of English life. A growing power struggle was developing between the king and the church. In 1164, Henry issued a document known as the Constitutions of Clarendon that formally documented the king's powers. The articles included the official right to try clergy members in royal courts instead of courts of the church.[29] This led to continued increased royal authority. However, it did not last very long.

Various political changes throughout the twelfth and thirteenth centuries reduced the king's control and resulted in the decline of feudalism in England. Significant events from this time include the signing of the Magna Carta, which increased the power of nobles at the expense of the king.

In 1215, tensions between nobles and the king reached a boiling point. Though better off than all the lower classes, the nobles were taxed highly and under constant fear of being jailed. The king at the time was King John, the youngest son of Henry II. John raised taxes even further, abused the law's powers by arresting all of his enemies, and fought with the church.

The nobles were growing increasingly unhappy, leading to a forced meeting with the king. This meeting resulted in the Magna Carta, an agreement where the king agreed to follow common laws, including respecting the traditional rights of nobles and barons, even involving them and church officials when considering special additional taxes. A key pact within the Magna Carta was that the king agreed that no person could be jailed without a trial. This was the defining principle of what would become an essential concept in English law known as *habeas corpus*.

By the 1300s, the first form of the English Parliament came to be. Parliament gave a modest form of power and representation even to commoners—meaning people of the lower class. This century represented a significant fall in the feudal state's control, allowing for more power to be spread among the people.

PLAGUE AND REBELLION

HOWEVER, A DESTRUCTIVE force would devastate much of the developed continent in the form of the Black Death. First appearing in the mid-1300s, the plague caused death and economic destruction throughout both Asia and Europe. The epidemic caused levels of death that seem unfathomable by any single cause today. It is estimated that nearly half of the population of both China and Europe died due to the plague.[30] During this period of disease, trade and commerce halted rapidly. Life could not go on as it had.

The plague represented a turning point for the medieval economy. Nobody was safe from the illness the plague caused. While nobles were able to hide in the luxury of their homes, peasants could not. The supply of necessary goods, such as food, became an issue. Since so many people died from the plague, there were not nearly as many workers as before.

Following this, there was not as much food as there had been. Since nobles and elites were not growing food themselves, they became dependent on the workers. Before the plague, nobles were not as reliant in quite the same way. In healthy times, while the lower classes were still the growers of food, the total supply of food grown was plentiful enough that the lower class could not exert leverage on the nobles. With the massive supply shock that resulted from the pandemic, food was now in short supply. The workers who survived were able to parlay the shortage of food into demands for more money and more rights.

As a result of all of this, many peasant rebellions broke

out once the plague subsided (although there were numerous waves of the plague). Nobles were not able to restore the balance to what it had been previously. This type of rebellion occurred all over Europe as well. England, France, Germany, Spain, and Italy all faced similar revolts because of the plague. While the rebellions were only modestly successful at points, the economies of these regions changed in a significant way. Through increased power, markets began to flourish as there was less direct control and taxation of the lower class's crops. The plague, however, coincided with the Hundred Years' War between France and England. The war was not kind to the lowest class. As with many wars before it, many of the problems were due to the money.

THE EFFECTS OF FUNDING WAR

THE HUNDRED YEARS' War is commonly described as the intermittent conflict between France and England from 1337 to 1453. The war was predominantly a struggle about land. While England legally ruled some of the land sitting in modern France, the French decided to push back. England was at a strategic and numerical disadvantage in this war for many reasons. Not only was France more highly populated and well financed, but England required ships to reach France and wage their defense.

England won many battles throughout the more than hundred years, but eventually it became too difficult for England's forces to maintain their stronghold on the land in French territory. France was able to force away and defeat English soldiers and resumed its status as a dominant force in Europe. The war did not end with a formal treaty. Instead, the English simply no longer sent soldiers to fight.

The financial aspect of the Hundred Years' War must

be noted as a factor in its eventual outcome. England was operating under the early implementation of its parliamentary system throughout the later stages of the war, which restricted the king's power so that he could not finance the war through any action he saw fit. As the ruler of England, the king wished to wage war at all costs—and could previously do so. Parliament, with a different mandate, had to approve each time the king needed more money to fund the war. While Parliament usually agreed to fund the wars further, there were often lengthy discussions and debates regarding the requests.

In France, there was no check on the power of the monarchy. Since the king did not need to consult his legislative assembly on any issues, such as taxation and funding for the war, he could enact policies at will, with the sole focus being to win all battles against England. While the power of the monarchy was falling in England, it was strengthening in France. New taxes were levied regularly in France as the king increased his war chest significantly. One of these taxes, the salt tax, remained in place for hundreds of years before being abolished in the eighteenth century.[31]

To enforce these taxes, a slew of new government jobs were opened as new tax collectors, record keepers, and mediators for disagreements needed to be hired to manage the system, which was increasing rapidly in scope. In essence, this was the first rudimentary form of today's Internal Revenue Service.

There is an interesting and noteworthy juxtaposition here. While still ruled by a monarchy, England was operating under far more democratic principles than France, due to its Parliament. Kings and rulers have shown throughout history that they will wage war at all costs to expand or keep their power. However, since England had a parliamentary system, there was a check on the king's power that was not present in France. While this sounds like a good thing, there are trade-offs to a system with checks and balances. One such negative balance appears during times of war.

Wars are won through swift and decisive decisions and rely on significant funding. A strong monarchy, such as France's, was able to make rapid decisions and utilize the power of the purse at a moment's notice. England's Parliament, which required meetings and debates to fund new taxes, lagged. Given that France already had a geographic advantage, the fact that England was also slower in swift decision making was likely a crucial factor in its eventual defeat.

However, part of why this is interesting can be seen by examining the short and long-term effects from the two different approaches of England and France. France undoubtedly benefited in the short term—its ability to win the war—from its strong monarchy, but that benefit came at a critical long-term cost. By minting as much new money as possible, combined with excessively high taxation, France devalued their currency and crippled their economy to win the war.

While France may have been able to gain territory from England, they had to sacrifice their post-war economy to do it. Not only were French citizens burdened by extremely high taxes, but many towns and villages were also ravaged by mercenary soldiers who forcibly claimed supplies to fuel their battles. These downsides are a direct effect of lengthy wars that are often driven by whirring up the printing presses and monetary mints. These outcomes can be seen still to this day, and the effects of war on currency and the economy will be explored in more detail later in this book.

MODERN BANKING
BEGINS

A s society progressed in the decades and centuries following the Hundred Years' War, and the world transitioned from the Middle Ages to the early modern period, a shift in the development of monetary systems occurred. The emergence of credit and debt saw money begin to expand in a way unlike at any earlier point in history. A system of credit allows users of money to avoid the constraints that come with a system where capital is required to be paid in full at all times.

Credit had been used before, with its first widespread uses being recorded in ancient Mesopotamia, and credit money had taken many various forms. While these monetary tools were indeed available and used at times, up to this point those instruments had tended to serve niche purposes, only used by small groups of people. Credit as money had never been prevalent throughout a large economy. While available as a financial tool, it was neither commonly accepted nor used.

MONEY WAREHOUSES

Since standard coinage had functioned reasonably well throughout the Middle Ages, with many countries basing their currencies on the superior metals of gold and silver, it would take a significant displacement for the structure of money itself to shift. This disruption occurred with the development of modern banks. Banks have appeared at numerous points throughout history—from ancient Egypt's early grain banking system to the more developed methods in Greece and Rome. These early banking institutions' primary purpose was to accept deposits from the public or the nobles and store the deposits safely. While lending did occur, it was not the defining purpose of these early banks. These banks functioned primarily as money warehouses and were places where the public could safely store their wealth and valuables.

Compared to the earliest banks, modern banking was a different beast altogether. The key differentiation separating modern banks from their previous equivalents had to do with actual ownership of money. With the early banks, the depositor was still the legal owner of the money. The depositors left their money in the bank for protection, but they still held ownership over their funds. This was not the case with the development of modern banking, just as it is not the case today.

When depositors put their funds into a bank system today, the money is now legally owned by the bank, not the depositor. The depositor, instead, receives a debt from the banks. The difference may seem small, but the impact is significant. Because of this change, banks became freed from many of the restrictions they were forced to be accountable to when they acted as money warehouses. Instead of protecting and storing depositor's funds, they now only had to fulfill the promise of the customer's debt that their funds will be available if they chose to withdraw them. This subtle but significant difference became increasingly common with banking institutions towards the latter period of the Middle Ages.

When considering the progression of banks from money storage to debt issuance, one must realize that the money issued by a bank was not commodity money at all. Instead, what was issued at that time was pure credit money, debt from the bank itself. Like other money, it could be traded and used for payment of goods and services. Through loans, banks issued debt without receiving corresponding deposits, essentially expanding the money supply.

While there had been primitive versions of credit money in the past, there was one crucial difference that was new to modern banking—the ability to return the credit and withdraw precious metals at a moment's notice. This capability resulted in a feeling of security from the banks' users, knowing that the bank receipt was truly one step away from owning the precious metal themselves. Banks were largely able to deliver on this, meaning it was quite rare for a bank to not have enough precious metal on hand to satisfy customer demand.

This stability and reliability were mostly due to the reputation of a bank, which played a large part in its popularity. If there was even one instance where a bank failed to meet a customer's demand to exchange a bank debt for metal money, the bank's reputation would be irreparably destroyed. Still, bank failures did occur at times. In moments of economic uncertainty, when a high number of people went to withdraw their metals from the banks at once—a bank run—insolvent banks would be exposed and fail.

A key development took place in 1694 in England, when a group of private interests received approval to create a bank that was specifically designed to lend to the government. This bank, called the Bank of England, would print the bank liabilities onto paper, which were then lent to the government. The breakthrough with banknote money came from the fact that England's government used these notes to pay its vendors and suppliers of goods.

Using banknotes to pay vendors allowed bank money to spread much further than it had ever gone before. Furthermore, since there was so much banknote money now flowing to the government vendors, those vendors demanded that the government accept those banknotes when collecting taxes. The government agreed, which meant that Bank of England banknotes were the only money besides coinage allowed for tax payments. Allowing banknotes to be used for tax payments was critical to the acceptance of paper money and established these banknotes' legitimacy.

CONTEMPORARY BANKING INSTITUTIONS

IT WAS HERE that banks began to take on the role that we think of today when we think of banks. The business model for banking institutions slowly evolved explicitly to create new money through debt. Where previously there were establishments that gave loans, now banking was an industry where providing loans was *the business*. Accepting deposits from depositors became a means to issue new circulating money in the form of loans.

This system presented a risk to the depositors of these banks. While today, governments guarantee bank users' deposits in the event that a bank fails, this was not the case when this form of banking became common. With most banks operating under a fractional reserve system—where the amount of money a bank held in reserves was less than the number of deposits made at the bank—there was an increased risk for bank clients who wanted solely to store their wealth safely and were not interested in loans or debt.

Notes issued by banks rapidly grew to be the most common medium of exchange in Britain during the seventeenth century, with much of the world following within the next one hundred years. With all these banks operating under a fractional reserve system, the supply of new money created was increased at rates not seen in hundreds of years. This represents another significant turning point in the story of money.

The main reason that paper money succeeded was because of its portability. Instead of needing to carry around purses of coins, light paper could easily be transferred. The downside, however, is the loss of scarcity. Modern money, meaning fiat money, traded away scarcity for portability. The history of money up until this point has been a slow march of humanity progressing towards the understanding that scarcity was the key factor for what makes good money, as long as the scarce asset is sufficiently divisible. With the onset of paper money, that link had been severed, though not quite fully broken.

In 1776, Adam Smith estimated that over three-quarters of the total money circulating in his homeland of Scotland was in the form of banknotes. It was no longer just one bank per region issuing currency, as it was at first with the Bank of England. There were now regional commercial banks operating independently to provide debt and banknote money. Since in England the two forms of money that were accepted remained coinage or specifically Bank of England notes, regional bank money was a credit that was convertible into one of these two monies. What this means is that you could pay your taxes with Bank of England bills, but not with local bank money. This system of money and banking spread throughout the European continent like wildfire.

The Bank of England represented an early model for

what central banks still do today. The bank became irrevo-cably linked to its government and became a crucial man-ager of the entire currency's supply. It was not until the Bank Charter Act of 1844 that absolute control over the money supply was exerted. The English government elected to elim-inate banknotes by regional banks, therefore enacting total central control over the nation's currency. This action lim-ited the amount of new money created, with the intention being to reduce inflation. While banknotes were required to be backed by either gold or government debt, the govern-ment retained the power to suspend this in times of financial crisis. As has been seen in many cases throughout history, arbitrary restrictions on money issuance tend not to last, happening in this case three times in the twenty-five years following the legislation.

While private banks were not allowed to issue notes of their own, they were still allowed to supply loans, increasing the currency supply. This model was akin to what we still see today, where a bank issues a loan, typically to fund a par-ticular investment, and new money is created. When that loan is paid back with interest, that new money is essentially destroyed. This form of currency creation became increas-ingly common. While only 10% of the money supply came from loans in England in 1800, it had reached 55% by 1844 and 85% by 1913, making debt the dominant form of new currency production. Today, this number is 97%.[32]

In this era, money started to evolve into the form that we recognize today, a credit banknote-based system. It would still take a few more centuries for money to transform into the fully fiat-based system that exists today, but the stage had been set. Banknote money had become normalized as a medium of exchange. Members of the public were willing to accept money that had no actual worth of its own because of the promise that the debt was convertible into the precious metals they knew to be valuable. What began with the Bank of England spread throughout the world, with other countries following suit one by one, issuing banknotes to represent a certain amount of metal held in a banking institution. Paper and bills became normalized as the way to transfer money from person to person.

Banknote money certainly has particular benefits over exchanging metal coins, with the most obvious being portability and the ability to control currency. When metal was the medium of exchange, central banks and governments had somewhat limited control over the money. Yes, currency mints would be under government control, but there was still a limit to how much currency could be produced because of the scarcities of the metals themselves. In a banknote money system, the issuance and denomination of bills could much more easily be manipulated.

Not everything about banknote paper money is superior to using metals, however. One of the biggest takeaways from the history of money is that people and societies have always naturally gravitated towards the forms of money that are the scarcest—provided that the money is sufficiently divisible, durable, portable, and recognizable. Scarcity in money has been the most reliable indicator of the success of civilizations throughout history and is often the crucial differentiator between societies that thrived and those that failed. With the onset of paper money, the progression towards scarcity that had occurred throughout the 13,000-year history of money had ceased. Instead of scarcity, portability and the ability to control the supply have become the defining traits of money. As will be seen throughout the remainder of this book, this has consequences.

WAMPUM AND THE COLONISTS

W HEN THE FIRST European settlers found their way to the American shores, life was challenging. Not only were they in unfamiliar territory, but civilization as they knew it had to be started from scratch essentially. Houses needed to be built, food needed to be grown or hunted, and there was no source of comfort to remind settlers of home.

Life was hard for the early colonists at first. Trade was essentially nonexistent for many years, as the pilgrims struggled to survive. There was barely enough food for survival. As such, for the early years, there was little need for money. Societies eventually began to stabilize and grow, however, and so too did the need for trade.

Barter was essentially the system at this time, with animal pelts, tobacco, and nails being goods that were frequently exchanged. As European-settled lands continued to grow, the need for a better form of money to conduct trade became increasingly necessary, yet the Europeans had no good options. There was no source of precious metals yet found in America, nor were there established banks to issue paper notes. Instead, it was the indigenous Americans who introduced the Europeans to the first proper money of the settlers' American experience.

NORTH AMERICAN MONEY

THE EASTERN WOODLANDS tribes used shell beads, known as "wampum," as their money. To make wampum required handcrafting shell beads from either the North Atlantic channeled whelk shell or the western North Atlantic hard-shelled clam. Cylindrical beads were crafted and placed on strings. Creating the Wampum beads was painstaking and laborious, which gave the money the level of scarcity required to succeed as money.

The shells needed to create wampum were only found in the Atlantic Ocean, but through trade, wampum managed to extend its reach far inland. Even though they were not a coastal tribe, the Iroquois managed to own the largest collection of wampum among all the indigenous tribes.[33] There were only a few tribes that had the combination of geographic proximity and skill set to specialize in the production of wampum.

Wampum was used both ceremoniously and as a general medium of exchange as well. Many tribes used it as a means to confirm political or religious measures. White shells represented peace and purity, while purple shells were often used in more serious matters, such as death and war. When two tribes met together to discuss an important arrangement, wampum was often exchanged to seal the agreement. Wampum was also given as gifts or exchanged on many varied occasions, including the birth of a child, marriage, and the signing of treaties.

As soon as European colonists reached American shores, an immediate problem regarding money became apparent. While much of Europe was using coins for money, there was not enough coinage in the newly colonized America. The English Crown relished this. Instead of paying colonists in coins for the supplies they shipped to England, the Crown paid the colonists with new supplies required to keep them working.[34] Even though they were an ocean apart, this closed-loop economy benefited the Crown at the expense of the colonists.

The colonists recognized the problem, a need for money, but it took them a while before realizing the solution was in front of them—wampum. Since colonists were used to money being made of metal coins, they had difficulty grasping the value of the indigenous bead money they saw in colonial New England. Functionally, wampum was not unlike European currencies. Wampum fulfilled the properties of money—divisibility, durability, portability, recognizability, and scarcity—quite well, but there was still hesitation among early European settlers. To them, only a metal coin with the face of a ruler stamped on it qualified as *real* money.

This bias regarding what constitutes *real* is not uncommon, but it is misguided. Especially in the modern era, users of money tend not to question their own money of choice, yet would be highly suspicious of being told that anything different was money. Instead, money should be analyzed according to whether or not it adequately fulfills the five properties of money and how it meets money's three functions. Not only was wampum reasonably scarce, but the beads made from shells were also exceptionally durable, allowing them to be transferred without fear of breaking.

Once the colonists moved past their hang-ups about wampum as money, they began to embrace it wholeheartedly. Wampum became a widespread form of money among colonists, who eventually used it without hesitation, trading with it regularly. On October 18, 1650, wampum was officially recognized as legal tender by the Massachusetts Bay Colony.[35] Before long, wampum was adopted as an official currency in all thirteen colonies. With an economy that operated predominantly using wampum, trade in the colonies flourished to a degree that had not previously occurred since they first landed on the American shores. Not only used among colonists, wampum was an ideal currency for trade with the indigenous Americans since both groups valued the beads.

COINS REPLACE WAMPUM

IN THE LATE 1600s, the beginning of the end of wampum had arrived. There are two reasons for this. First, the British Crown had given in over its complete control over gold and silver and allowed for more coins to be shipped overseas to the Americas. The colonists finally had access to the types of money they had always been comfortable with, and many wampum users would switch back to using coins. The monetary properties of gold and silver coins were superior to that of wampum. Coins were both more durable and scarcer. The emergence of coin circulation in the Americas resulted in the natural progression to better money, as has happened in human society throughout history.

Compounding this further was the development of mass-production techniques used by the colonists to produce more wampum. While not possible at first, the colonists eventually learned how to make wampum beads using quick and effective manufacturing techniques that were more advanced than what the indigenous Americans had. This increased manufacturing led to new wampum being created rapidly, reducing its scarcity and value. Wampum continued to be used as an occasional medium of exchange, even into the twentieth century, but its use declined significantly. Wampum went from being the dominant medium of exchange to one that was mainly used for novelty purposes or as jewelry or decoration.

Money that is difficult to produce makes for higher-quality money because scarcity is arguably the most important factor in determining a currency's lifespan. Money that is provably scarce but difficult to transport—such as Rai stones—will generally survive longer than a money that is too abundant. The best form of money usually wins. Wampum worked very well as money for the early colonists, and its demise came from a common factor that has been seen with many types of money throughout history—once someone figures out how to mass-produce the money, that money is on its last legs.

There is an interesting trend that has occurred throughout much of history, a monetary oscillation of sorts. At first, when a new money or currency becomes popular, there is a shortage of the money, with there simply not being enough to go around. The swing occurs later, once the means to quell the shortage of currency is realized. At that point, hyperinflation rapidly occurs. There is rarely much time spent in the Goldilocks zone, meaning the perfect amount of new money minted. There is typically either not enough currency or too much.

This was the case with early coinage in the Americas as well. While coins became used with more frequency, there remained a limit on the number of new coins that were available. As expansion in the colonies moved westward, coinage was difficult to come by. This effect was compounded by the natural behaviors that result from such a currency shortage. Since users of the currency knew that it would be difficult to acquire more currency, they become reluctant to spend what they already had. This reduction in how often currency is exchanged—known as the "velocity of money"—intensified the shortages even further.

Additional frustration among the colonists was caused by the fact that they were forced to use British coins and could not mint their own money due to restrictions by the British government. This lack of permission to issue their own gold and silver coins was partly what led the colonies to be more receptive to paper money than was common in many European countries. The first paper banknotes arrived in the Massachusetts Bay Colony in 1690. These notes were redeemable for gold and silver and could be used for tax payment purposes.

PAPER REPLACES COINS

OTHER STATES BEGAN to follow this model and started to issue paper notes. The issuance was a problem, however, as most states quickly created more paper banknotes than there were available reserves of precious metal. This is the classic issue with paper money, and it is an issue that remains true today. A government or minting body cannot issue more value. Money itself is not value. Instead, it is the tool that allows us to *obtain* the item of value that we want. The government can only choose to devalue a currency by minting more of it.

Said another way, issuing more paper bills does not create any additional value for society. Money is a neutral tool for measurement. When additional currency is issued, no new goods are created in an economy. Since money is a tool to measure the value of goods and services against one another, the price of goods and services rises when new money is issued.

Governments and central banks often overlook this concept. Instead of looking at money as a neutral tool for measurement, equivalent to a clock, thermometer, or ruler, money is viewed as a political tool, used to accomplish whichever tasks the ruling party chooses. Thinking with this perspective, often completely unaware of how systems of money function, the tool of money becomes manipulative in nature. The currency is issued to accomplish goals, unaware that the destruction of the monetary system itself is often the result.

This was the outcome with many states that issued paper notes. Over-issuance became such a problem that many of the states' notes became essentially worthless in a short time. Rhode Island issued its paper note in 1750, and by 1770 the currency had no value. Thus, the colonies remained an amalgam of various forms of money, with no one currency uniting throughout all states.

With the release of the Declaration of Independence and the onset of the Revolutionary War, careful monetary management was wholly disregarded. With no means to pay for battle, a trove of paper money was printed. This choice was made deliberately by the newly established American Congress, as there were only two other possibilities to raise funds, and both were flawed. The first would be to requisition goods and services directly. This has obvious problems and would result in diminishing returns to the eventual point that there would be no goods left to requisition. The second alternative would be taxation. Early Americans were not exactly fond of taxation, and to propose a tax to fund independence would have been difficult. As such, the chosen option was to issue new money at will to pay for goods.

And so it was that the Continental dollar came into issuance in 1776 and was used to fund the American Revolution. However, as has been previously discussed, paper money only holds its value when its issuance is carefully and conservatively managed to prevent high inflation. Since Continental dollars existed for the sole purpose of funding the Revolution, there was little chance that hyperinflation would not occur. While attempts were made to prevent rising prices, price controls tend to fail eventually. The Continental dollar lost value staggeringly quickly, with its value in 1781 being only worth 1/100th of its initial issuance value. Ultimately, the value fell even further, to 1/1000th of its original worth.[36] It did not take long for shopkeepers and merchants to refuse to accept Continental dollars, instead preferring more traditional media of exchange.

THE WILD WEST OF
BANKING

S INCE THE ISSUE of currency had been very problematic
throughout the Revolution, the topic of money needed
to be dealt with as soon as the war had reached its conclusion. The Constitutional Convention in 1787 began to
tackle this question, eventually reaching its climax with the
ratification of the Constitution in 1789. It was not until the
Coinage Act of 1792 that the dollar became the official
American currency. A vital characteristic of the Act was that
it formally established that the dollar would be bimetallic,
with one dollar equivalent to 371.25 grains of silver or 24.75
grains of gold. This decree established a formal valuation
method and linkage between gold and silver. The decision
was made so that the dollar would receive the benefits that
both gold and silver uniquely supply.

THE PROBLEMS WITH BIMETALLISM

WHEN USING GOLD as a currency, a nation can store wealth
best over time since gold is significantly scarcer than silver.
Using gold can be problematic, however. Since gold is scarce
and therefore valuable, it can be challenging to exchange
small values of it, as even a tiny quantity of gold can have a
high worth. Silver does not have the same level of scarcity
as gold. While this does reduce its store of value potential,
it allows silver to be superior to gold for low-value trans-

actions. This was the justification for pegging the dollar to both gold and silver.

In practice, a fixed link to both metals led to difficulties. First, newly minted coins were rapidly leaving circulation once they were issued. Americans preferred to keep their freshly minted coins and used older Spanish currency for most transactions, leading to issues because using foreign currencies was set out as illegal within the Constitution. After failing to resolve this issue, the law banning the use of foreign currencies was suspended for more than twenty-five years.

More problematic was the silver content of the US coins. At a ratio of 15:1 silver to gold, silver was slightly overvalued in US coins compared to both currencies overseas and the natural price on the market. Most coins in the US began to be made of silver, even though both gold and silver were intended to be used. A minter or bank could acquire sixteen ounces of silver on the market for one ounce of gold while only needing to use fifteen ounces of silver when minting coins. The disparity incentivized the use of silver over gold in the minting process.

This is part of the issue with attaching a currency to two different metals, such as gold and silver. While one hopes to achieve the desirable effects from using both metals, it is impossible to avoid the natural market forces that complicate bimetallism's practical use. Independent of the ratios used in the minting of coins, the prices of gold and silver move on their own, as market conditions for the metals shift. Since the price of these metals adjusts to shifts in supply and demand, the natural price ratios between the two metals change over time as well. Thus, it is impossible to maintain a fixed price between the two metals. When using a set rate between the two metals in the valuation of a coin, it is unavoidable that either gold or silver will be under or over-valued at any given point.

Throughout this time, banking in the US operated in a relatively free-for-all manner. Different states all used various methods of money and banking. Some states issued paper money, while others attempted to ban paper money completely and even to limit what banking services were allowed. There was also a segment of the population that wished for stricter regulations and well-defined paper money issuance. There was no standard throughout America in the first half of the nineteenth century, far from it. With little communication between many states, the possibility of encountering considerably different money standards was high for travelers and merchants between states.

The role of credit also became an essential yet difficult question to answer at this stage of American growth. Credit flowed easily and abundantly throughout the United States as the country grew and expansion continued to move westward. The economy of the country was growing at an exponential pace. There is a bit of a chicken and the egg dilemma regarding credit in the early US. Was it the availability of easy credit and debt that led to a roaring economic expansion? Or was it the rapid expansion of US growth that naturally led to the increase in credit? Both are likely true to some degree.

This growth lends credence, in some capacity, to the belief held by many in modern economics that it is beneficial to allow for higher credit levels to aid in the expansion of the economy, only to be reined in more tightly if credit begins to get out of control. Of course, this careful approach is often not so carefully managed, as has been seen with many cycles of debt and currency failure throughout history. The number of banks steadily grew in the US during this period, eventually reaching over 1,600 in 1861.[37]

While the first half of the nineteenth century was characterized by anything-goes banking, with a decentralized nature and lack of cohesion, the latter half of the century began to swing back to a more centralized and disciplined national banking system. The onset of the Civil War required a monetary cohesion that was not possible under the chaotic banking system that had been present up to that point.

THE CIVIL WAR'S IMPACT

THE WAR LED to the first income tax in America in 1861, alongside a bevy of other taxes and tariffs, which were a first for the previously tax-resisting American population. As the Civil War began, the convertibility of banknotes to precious metals quickly became broken and later suspended. Both the North and the South altered banknote convertibility.

Compared to one another, the South was much more active at the printing press than the North. It was more difficult to collect taxes in the South due to its population's more geographically diverse nature, although this was a minor factor in the South's willingness to expand their monetary base. The South was willing to finance the war by any means necessary, which necessarily meant printing as many new paper notes as possible. In the four years from 1861 to 1865, it is estimated that the South expanded their money supply by over eleven times.

While this type of monetary expansion may allow a government to fund an action such as a war, there are consequences to this uninhibited money printing. Knowing that their currency's value was depreciating, Southerners were quick to use their money, essentially keeping as little money saved as possible. This behavior is rational and harkens back to the lessons from the early stages of monetary development. If a form of money cannot hold value over time, users of the currency are incentivized to spend the money as quickly as possible to prevent the loss in purchasing power of their savings. This is what occurred in the South as the monetary base rapidly expanded.

Combined with the immense growth in the money supply was the reduction in the production of goods. Since many workers were brought into war and productive land was often destroyed as a casualty of the battles, there was lesser production of many goods. A falling number of goods combined with a rising money supply is a recipe for high or hyperinflation, which is precisely what occurred in the South. It is estimated that prices rose by twenty-eight times during the Civil War.[38]

By comparison, the North experienced much more mild inflation, with prices only rising by about two times by the end of the war. The North had tremendous advantages over the South in this area, with a production capacity that was not possible in the South. Most of the US's railways were located in the North, and the North had more than twice the population level. Even if the South had managed its fiscal policies differently, there would likely still have been higher inflation than in the North simply due to the difference in production ability between the two regions.

With the South having seceded from the country, the North was free to nationalize currency however they saw fit. The action taken was through the issuance of greenbacks, established by the Legal Tender Act in 1862. Greenbacks were a fiat currency, meaning that they were not representative of any precious metal. The money was the paper itself.

While they were formally named "United States Government Notes," the currency took on the informal name "greenbacks" because of the distinct green color on one side of the bill. Greenbacks were issued numerous times throughout the remaining years of the war and were accepted as legal tender.

NATIONAL AND STATE BANKING IS BORN

GREENBACKS WERE ALWAYS intended to be temporary, however, used solely for the Civil War. When the war ended, there was a strong divide in the country over the currency's efficacy. This was the beginning of the national and state banking system that is still known today. For state banks to issue notes, they were required to purchase bonds from the government in amounts that met specific capital requirements. The result was an expanded market for the issuance of bonds that also allowed the states to issue a unified banknote that was generally accepted everywhere.

There were still states issuing their own notes, however. Banks in each state were allowed to continue to issue their own notes, while new banks had the option of partnering with the national bank to issue national notes. Since the governments preferred using the national notes, they imposed a 2% tax on state banknote issuance, which was later raised to 10%. While not making state banknotes illegal, they were effectively taxed out of everyday use.

Alongside the development of American banking, with the transition from state-only banks to the dual national and state system, came a fierce debate about the use of money. More specifically, the Civil War brought to the surface intense discussion regarding how money should work, namely concerning the use of gold, silver, and the convertibility of paper notes to both of those metals. Bimetallism is fatally flawed after all, as discussed earlier.

A problem that arose quite regularly in these discussions was the idea of a capital flight of coins from one country to another, depending on the bimetallic standard used.

For example, the US might peg its paper note to a ratio of gold/silver at a different rate than a country such as France was using. The difference would naturally lead to a currency arbitrage, where there was an outflow of precious metal from the country with a lesser gold ratio to the country with a more favorable one. This arbitrage of exchange is what led the US to change its ratio in 1832.

After the end of the Civil war, bimetallism was on its last legs, with the US and France being the two major countries operating on a bimetallic standard. Both countries were reluctant to give up using silver for the primary reason that using both metals allowed for a larger supply of currency, since both metals could be used instead of solely drawing on the scarcer gold. There were attempts to coordinate fixed ratios between multiple countries; however, the currencies still would have been arbitraged due to natural market forces. If gold and silver were mined at a ratio different than, for example, 1:15, then one metal would naturally be overvalued while the other would be undervalued. The impossibility of maintaining pegged, dual rates is why a bimetallic system does not work.

Because of this, sentiment within the United States regarding silver quickly fell in the period after the Civil War. This feeling was particularly true in cities, where the fear of inflation drove gold to be the prevalent metal used in reserves. While this was happening, however, silver maintained a level of support and use in the expanding West and parts of the South. In a way, there was another war brewing between the gold users of cities and the silver users in rural areas. This eventually became a significant economic policy debate for the remainder of the eighteenth century, known as the "free silver" movement.

"Free silver" was the belief among many, particularly silver miners, that an unlimited amount of silver coins should be allowed to be minted and sold on the market, essentially allowing for currency to be issued as quickly as silver could be mined. This approach was in stark contrast to the limited currency issuance that utilized a more conservative gold standard. While it was evident that allowing for unlimited silver coins to be issued would be inflationary and raise prices, free silver advocates were aware of this fact and believed it would benefit the economy. Employing similar logic used today with modern money, the free silver movement thought that the currency's devaluation would allow farmers to benefit from their crops' higher prices while also allowing debts to be reduced in real terms.

Free silver was trendy among populist organizations that favored reductions in the credit burden that the policy would bring. Eventually, the free silver cause could not find enough support in cities, and the country continued to head towards a fully gold-based currency.

Simultaneously, the battle between gold and silver waged on as the ongoing debate about greenbacks continued. A new political party known as the "Greenback Party" was formed in 1875, arguing that the nation should fully shift to a monetary standard of paper notes with no backing. The party argued along similar lines as the free silver movement that prices should rise further than gold would allow. While the party did offer presidential candidates in three elections, they did not receive much electoral support, garnering only a few percentage points of the vote. However, the party did have its share of supporters among the public and managed to elect a dozen or so members to Congress.

While gold was the dominant form of money in the United States as the century came to an end, there was disagreement and debate among the populace about the role money should play in the economy. With the onset of paper money in the form of greenbacks, Americans had become exposed to the concept of paper money in a new and unique way. At the same time, gold presents obvious limits when being used as a currency.

Gold is scarce to the degree that it prevents those who wish to expand and control the money from doing so to the extent that they would like, though it can be argued that these limits are a good thing. Regardless, the fact remained that there was an increasing dissatisfaction with respect to money in the country, evidenced by the point that today in 2020, gold is no longer the basis for any national currency in the world. Consequently, it is here in the 1800s that America began on its path towards the modern fiat monetary system that exists today.

Still, US money became quite a great deal more sophisticated throughout the 1800s. After becoming free of British rule, the country rapidly advanced its institutions of money and banking. Money was becoming increasingly centralized, with state-only and private banknotes being pushed out in favor of the new dual banking system at the federal and state level. Money's centralization is a key theme to remember, as it is a trend that continues from here.

THE BIRTH OF THE
FEDERAL RESERVE

W ITH THE PASSAGE of the Gold Standard Act in
1900, gold formally became established as the only
metal for which paper notes could be redeemed, putting a
defined end to the era of bimetallism that had been in effect
for the century prior. Economically, gold was already the
majority's preferred metal at this point, but it was in 1900
that paper notes were officially no longer convertible for silver. On its own, choosing gold alone would seem to reduce
the ability of issuers to increase the money supply, since only
gold was required to be held in reserves. Still, the Act clev-
erly contained a number of provisions that allowed the supply of money to increase even beyond the rate that it had
when both metals were used.

Being on a gold standard was not enough to prevent
instability in the banking system. One problem was the tim-
ing of bank deposits in more rural areas of the country. In
these parts of the US, farming was the predominant work
for many people. For farmers, being geographically located
in the same general area as their neighbors meant that many
of these farmers' crops would grow on similar schedules.

Think about the typical structure of a bank. A bank must
keep a portion of the deposits it receives as reserves while
giving out the majority of depositor funds in the form of
loans. This method works well in many places, such as cities,
where different people regularly deposit funds. Even keeping

a small amount of cash in reserves typically allows a bank to fulfill any withdrawal requests that a customer could have. The system only fails when many customers desire to withdraw their funds at the same time. Since the bank has loaned out much of those deposits, there is not enough money to give to everyone who wishes to withdraw. This is what is known as a "bank run."

In parts of America where specific financial needs were often seasonal, this created difficulty for banks. Farmers would often deposit funds and request loans at similar times as their neighbors, which meant that they usually also desired to withdraw funds at the same time as one another. This led to many natural runs on the banks of sorts, except instead of it being caused by fear in the markets, they were driven by the natural seasonality that the clients' work required. The issue was that there was no lender of last resort, meaning no place where a bank itself could temporarily borrow funds from another bank that would be paid back at a later point in the seasonal banking cycle. The desire to address these problems, which more than a few banks suffered from—particularly after an especially large bank panic in New York in 1907—led to the creation of the nation's national bank, the Federal Reserve.

A BANK FOR BANKS

THE 1913 FEDERAL Reserve Act established a formal, national banking system where the Federal Reserve itself sat at the head. Twelve Federal Reserve districts were founded, with each district having its own Reserve Bank and numerous additional branches established in the larger districts. All national banks were required to join the system. The Federal Reserve Act established considerable powers for the newly created institution, chiefly being a bank for banks. National banks were required to store a share of their reserves at the reserve bank in their district.

The Federal Reserve itself is an independent body—meaning it operates separate from the government, although Federal Reserve governors are appointed by the President—with the task of managing the currency itself. This concept of having an apolitical (in theory) institution with the sole purpose of managing the nation's money is vitally important. As has been seen throughout history, one of the most common reasons that a currency fails is because it is minted or issued for purely political purposes. With it already being challenging to keep monetary systems successfully functioning over a long period without hyperinflation, the introduction of political gamesmanship into the issuance of the currency itself has nearly always eventually ended in disaster.

Thus, the Federal Reserve's chief role is to manage the US dollar while also being the lender of last resort to banks and being the bank of the government. To maintain the dollar, the Federal Reserve attempts to keep the economy stable and exercise the limits of its central banking power to prevent an economic downturn. Essentially, the Federal Reserve has three primary functions.

1. Manage the overall monetary policy of the US through the setting of interest rates and the money supply.
2. Be an effective payment rail for institutions like banks to pay each other.
3. Supervise the nation's banking operations as a whole.

The establishment of the Federal Reserve permanently

changed the nature of American money. Whereas a free-
for-all banking system was in place throughout much of the
1800s, with only limited federal intervention by the end of
the century, now there was a singular centralized body at the
helm of the entire nation's currency. There was certainly a
need for banking reform in the country, as runs on banks
and bank failures had become increasingly common in the
previous decade, yet the Federal Reserve's unelected members claimed a significant level of control over the most critical layer of the American economy—the money.

The Federal Reserve (also referred to as "the Fed") system
provides a certain level of stability for the economy and
the currency itself. Too often throughout history, monetary
issuance has been executed for personal or political gain. The
Fed also ensures that the nation's banks are operating with
sufficient capital requirements and can handle specific stress
tests that ensure the banks remain solvent even in times of
crisis. At the same time, the Fed is only held to a limited
degree of accountability. It is considered a privately-owned
central bank, even though the President appoints its board.
Its officials are unelected yet wield tremendous power within
the country.

WWI TESTS THE GOLD STANDARD

THE USE OF a gold standard worked well for American
money for a few years but was quickly tested with World
War I. As discussed throughout *The Story of Money*, war
is expensive, and currency devaluations are common when
wars occur. When World War I began, much of the world
was operating on a gold standard. This quickly ceased as
country after country suspended convertibility of their

paper money to gold so the supply of paper money could be increased to fund the ongoing war.

The US managed to continue convertibility longer than most nations, as long as it remained neutral in the war, but eventually, it too suspended convertibility. In fact, World War I almost eradicated the international gold standard. Countries did not demonize gold, nor did they even demonetize it. Instead, they quietly ignored the rates that were required to be held in terms of gold reserves to paper money issued. The suspension of the gold standard was always intended to be temporary, however. Indeed, all significant countries still recognized the need for gold to play an essential role in money issuance. It was not that the concept of a gold standard was obsolete. On the contrary, it was regarded as necessary.

Because so many countries deviated from the gold standard during the war, it was a significant struggle to restore the tie to gold at the war's conclusion. While individual countries had temporarily abandoned the gold peg previously, it was relatively easy to establish a link later by looking to an outside currency as a frame of reference. For example, if the US left its gold standard but England maintained its peg, the US could use England's peg to establish its own again. After World War I, this was not possible.[39]

Globally, years of price controls and massive shipments of gold internationally between nations thoroughly distorted the true market price for money, which made it impossible to determine the proper peg for paper money. Many governments wanted to return to the ratio of before, but this did not work in practice. Since significant amounts of new currency were printed to fund the war, it was impossible to return to a pre-war ratio since the paper money no longer held the value it had previously.

While many countries were scrambling to reinstate a proper gold standard, the US was comparatively stable, having avoided the severity of many of the negative consequences from the war that others faced. Although the US maintained its gold standard, the Federal Reserve was not significantly restricted in the amount of new currency that could be issued, as they held significant amounts of gold in reserve. This led to a policy of a highly expansionary monetary supply throughout the 1920s. As usually happens in times of loose credit, a large debt bubble formed, eventually popping with the Great Depression.

THE GREAT DEPRESSION TESTS IT FURTHER

THERE ARE MANY theories as to the cause of the Great Depression and the subsequent policies to bring the country out of it, but *The Story of Money* is not a textbook of American history. This book is about money and, as such, will stick to the monetary factors involved in the Depression.

The 1920s led to a sharp expansion of the money supply to fuel demand for debt that led to a reduction in the value of the dollar. This monetary supply surge did not lead to significant consumer-price-index (CPI) inflation—the traditional measure of inflation—meaning that prices of goods did not significantly rise.[40] This is because productivity in the 1920s skyrocketed due to new technologies and rapid improvements in the efficiency of manufacturing.

Money was easy to get in the 1920s and productivity rose, leading to ever-growing consumer confidence. When an economy is booming and there is an abundance of easy credit, the amount of debt in the economy begins to grow. Mounting debt does not cause immediate problems for the economy since debt is increasing alongside productivity growth and rising incomes, which mitigates many of the issues that result from escalating debt. Since incomes rise at a rate equal to or exceeding the swelling rate of debt, consumers can pay their debts with minimal issue.

The problems with debt surface when productivity slows and the growth in debt begins to outpace rising incomes. When this occurs, it is more challenging to pay off loans since the obligation becomes a higher and higher percentage of earnings. When debts cannot be paid through income alone, other financial assets such as stocks need to be sold off to pay what is owed, leading to the price of financial assets falling, which makes it harder for others to pay debts, and so forth. In short, once the growth of debt steadily outpaces the growth in incomes, a downward spiral occurs that sends the economy into recession. This is what ultimately led to the Great Depression.

The Federal Reserve was beginning to run into a problem towards the end of the 1920s as well. Since the Federal Reserve was limited in the number of paper notes it could print by the amount of gold it kept in reserves, the Fed naturally needed to continuously acquire new gold to fund its operations. Since the monetary policy of the 1920s was extremely expansionary, by the end of the decade the Fed was beginning to reach the limits of its ability to print new paper dollar notes.

This combination of the Great Depression occurring at the same time that the Federal Reserve was reaching its limits on its ability to create new dollars led to Executive Order 6102 by President Franklin Delano Roosevelt in 1933, which outlawed the private ownership of gold and required that all gold be turned in to a local Federal Reserve branch to be exchanged for a fixed rate of $20.67 per oz of gold.

The rationale for the order was that the "hoarding of gold" by private citizens hurt the economy by stalling growth, and thereby worsening the depression. The actual reason for Executive Order 6102 was that the government was running out of money and was lacking the gold needed in reserves to print more dollars.

This logic is dishonest, however, and there is no such thing as "hoarding" gold, as holding gold is merely a way to maintain savings. In the same way that it is not considered hoarding to keep dollars in a savings account, it is not hoarding to keep savings in the form of gold. Owning gold is the same principle as using a savings account, except using a different form of money.

The ethics of Executive Order 6102 deserve to be scrutinized. The rationale for the action was quite clear. Without confiscating the gold of individuals, the government could not spend what was needed to help bring the economy out of depression. Still, individuals holding gold were simply attempting to maintain their wealth in a period of significant economic collapse.

By mandating that people give up their gold—the protection of their savings—in an attempt to help the economy, President Roosevelt's order forced the small minority of Americans with the means to protect their wealth to suffer along the with rest of the flagging economy. This event was compounded further the very next year when the President raised the value of the confiscated gold to $35 per oz, as opposed to the previous $20.67, effectively devaluing the dollar by over 40%. It would be another forty years before Americans were legally allowed to hold gold again.

BRETTON WOODS AND THE DOLLAR

T HE EFFECTS FROM the Great Depression continued to be felt through the start of World War II, which significantly boosted the American economy. While the economies of nearly all European countries were devastated due to the war, the American economy became substantially stronger. GDP grew significantly, going from $209 billion in 1939 to $234 billion in 1947.[41]

Still, the war had been of such massive scope that it had completely thrown the world's currencies out of balance, like World War I before it. As the end of the war came in sight, with the Allied powers heading towards victory, the global financial system had been so completely mangled from warfare that it was deemed necessary to meet together to discuss the state of the post-war monetary system. This became the Bretton Woods Conference.

THE CONFERENCE

DELEGATES FROM MORE than forty nations joined together in Bretton Woods, New Hampshire, to discuss the future of money. Not only was the setting of exchange rates among the topics to be addressed, but there was also a desire to speak to a lack of cooperation among countries with regards to monetary policies. Since World War I ended, there had been numerous competitive devaluations among countries, lowering their exchange rates to incentivize a positive trade balance. When a country lowers its currency value, it becomes cheaper for other jurisdictions to buy that country's manufactured goods.

However, the downside is that savers are penalized when a country devalues its own currency. If you are someone with $1,000 in savings and your country engages in an international currency devaluation, your savings cannot buy as many foreign goods as the $1,000 was able to buy previously. This type of action is frequently carried out and even occurs quite often today. In fact, the currency devaluations that occurred in 2020 were far beyond the scope of what was done following World War I.

There was a desire for both flexibility and increased stability with the monetary system, though those tend to be at odds with one another. Fixed exchange rates between currencies were seen as necessary to prevent currency devaluations. While fixed rates did not work when the system of bimetallism was being used in the US, there was nonetheless the consensus that floating exchange rates would result in worse outcomes for trade. The result of the Bretton Woods Conference was that the US would be the only country to peg its currency to gold, while all other countries would link their currencies to the US dollar. This allowed for fixed exchange rates between countries that could be strategically adjusted while maintaining a generally stable rate with the dollar. There was no longer any appetite for the wild west of banking that dominated the 1800s.

Most developed countries agreed with the United States' vision of cooperative global economic management based on free trade, even though this arrangement strongly favored the US as the world's largest economic power. There was a push to establish more international trade and reduce the barriers and taxes that restricted it.

The idea was that by fixing nations' exchange rates to the US dollar, governments would not constantly be trying to tinker with their currencies to gain a trade advantage. Instead, by fixing exchange rates and focusing on establishing more free international trade, the role of monetary policy in the economy would be reduced and countries could focus their attention on strengthening their markets. In a way, the intent was to minimize the economic meddling and competitive devaluation that was regularly occurring between countries.

The Bretton Woods system also established several international organizations, such as the International Monetary Fund and the International Bank for Reconstruction and Development (IBRD), now the World Bank. Part of the reason for establishing these organizations was to prevent the closed trade systems that were commonly found in the 1930s, where countries would restrict trading with one another. International trade and economic globalization were now highly encouraged.

As it was, the world now operated on a quasi-gold standard, and the global economy worked quite well throughout its early years. There had been talk during Bretton Woods about creating a brand-new, international currency, tentatively called "Bancor," but the Americans were not willing to consider the idea. And so it was the dollar that became the reserve currency of the world.

Dollars were highly demanded by nations worldwide, particularly immediately in the period following World War II. There were massive trade surpluses in the US during this time, meaning that other countries were buying many more US goods than the US was buying international goods. The result was the US ran regular budget surpluses while many European nations faced significant deficits. To resolve this, an act known as the Marshall Plan was enacted in 1947 that allowed European countries to devalue their currencies against the dollar to balance trade.

THE US DOLLAR BECOMES THE STANDARD

UNDER BRETTON WOODS, the dollar was the only currency that was convertible to gold. The fact that the dollar maintained its convertibility meant that foreign nations were permitted to exchange their dollars for US gold reserves if they desired a fixed rate of $35 per ounce of gold. However, this is complicated to maintain since there was still an international gold market outside of currency markets, meaning that direct convertibility for dollars was not the only way that a nation could acquire gold.

Prices for all goods are determined based on supply and demand. For readers without an economics background, a simple way to understand what supply and demand mean in real terms is "people who are willing to make stuff" and "people who are willing to buy stuff." Where those two sides meet in the middle determines the price of a good or service.

Since gold had an international market outside of currency convertibility, the gold price on the free market needed to be at or near the fixed $35/oz for US dollar convertibility. If the price were different, an arbitrage opportunity would present itself. When the price of free-market gold was below $35/oz, it would make sense for nations to buy gold on the market, convert it to dollars at $35/oz, and profit from the exchange. Similarly, if the gold price were above $35, it would make sense to convert gold at the lower

$35/oz price and then sell it on the open market for more. This type of arbitrage is part of why attempting to fix the price of a good rarely succeeds.

Part of what the Bretton Woods system achieved was the internationalization of banking, where countries worked together in various aspects to manage currencies and achieve banking partnerships. Many of the largest banks established bases in multiple territories for the first time as the world became more globalized. This period is when foreign currency markets began developing comprehensive strategies to hedge the risks involved in exchange rate trends and fluctuations. Since countries were reluctant to alter exchange rates unless truly necessary, the fixed official exchange rates often varied from the market's demands. With banking infrastructure having advanced significantly, large capital flows were possible in ways that were previously difficult or impossible, leading to destabilized markets in many jurisdictions.

BRETTON WOODS CRUMBLES

IN THE DECADES following the beginning of Bretton Woods, the United States began to lose its dominant market share of the global economy as powers in Europe and Japan recovered from the war and became international economic powers. This shift away from US dominance towards a more diverse world economy led to increasing dissatisfaction with the US dollar's unique role as the *de facto* world currency. Due to the dollar's status, US policy was highly influential in the economic conditions of international countries. For the countries with strong economies of their own, this influence was not always welcome.

The dollar's strength began to fall in the 1960s as US President Lyndon B. Johnson chose to pay for the Vietnam

War through money issuance instead of a tax. As new currency was minted to fund the war, with that currency then flowing out of the country, the dollar's strength naturally weakened. However, in a fixed-exchange-rate world, the official rates between the dollar and other currencies did not change. This led to a situation where official dollar exchange rates were overvalued compared to their true market exchange rates, which incentivized foreign countries to hold other currencies. As has been illustrated numerous times already, fixed exchange rates cannot work over a long period as the market demands naturally shift over time.

As President Richard Nixon took office in 1969, the Bretton Woods system was beginning to crack. There was a continued outflow of dollars from the US to international markets, and large public debt had accrued as a result of the Vietnam War. There was also increasing price inflation of consumer goods within the US that had the additional effect of causing the dollar to become overvalued compared to the strongest international currencies. The US was steadily losing gold reserves due to the overvalued dollar convertibility, and the entire structure of the US currency and economy was beginning to fall apart.

On August 15, 1971, President Nixon formally suspended dollar convertibility, essentially ending the Bretton Woods system. At this point, the gold standard was officially abandoned. With this action by the US, paper notes became the standard form of money around the world.

Two years after convertibility was suspended, the system of fixed exchange rates ended as well. Now it was again up to each country to choose how to manage its currency supply. This floating exchange rate system is still used today. While floating exchange rates are superior to the impossible reality of fixed exchange rates, floating rates always result in numerous challenges for competing nations.

It was here in 1971 that gold lost its monetary status in the United States. Abandoning the gold standard was a massive and hugely significant change to how the US dollar functioned as a currency, which unquestionably shifted the US economy's direction for the next half-century. Yet, to the average American, nothing changed with the suspension of gold convertibility. The dollars in their pockets still bought the same groceries that they did before. Even today, the significance of President Nixon ending the Bretton Woods system is rarely discussed. As we will see, however, actions have consequences.

THE FIAT ERA BEGINS

WHEN PRESIDENT NIXON ended the convertibility of the US dollar to gold in 1971, the entire world lost its link to gold as money. Since foreign currencies had rates that were fixed to the US dollar and the US dollar was fixed to gold, all international currencies operated on a standard defined by gold as well.

There was only one difference between how money worked in the US before and after the gold standard was ended. Whereas on the gold standard, there had been a cap on the number of US dollars that could be created, there was no longer any limit. There could be as many dollars as the central bank and the government wanted.

THE IMPERCEPTIBLE SWITCH

THE KEY TO a successful fiat monetary policy is a combination of discipline and a strict operating framework. While the average person might believe that paper money has no value in itself, and that the only value comes from a collective social agreement that paper can be money, this is not strictly true. Money has specific properties, and it is the degree to which a form of currency meets those traits that will determine how well a money will work. A government-issued paper money is divisible, portable, and counterfeit resistant. An ordinary person is not capable of creating fake money. These qualities alone give paper money genuine value. The key for paper money to work or not, however, rests on how its scarcity is managed.

The role of scarcity as a crucial trait in the quality of money is absolutely critical yet poorly understood. Besides natural causes, such as plague and famine, and outside other human actions such as warfare, hyperinflation is by far the most common human-driven and political reason that societies collapse. For a fiat money system to succeed, the currency must be carefully managed so that hyperinflation does not occur.

To most Americans, nothing changed on the day that dollar convertibility to gold was suspended. To them, money continued to work as it always had. Money was always paper, so what was the difference whether it was backed by gold or not?

A misunderstood view is that using paper money is an advancement in money, the next and obvious evolution from metals. However, as we have seen before, paper money as a concept is not new; its roots date back to ancient China. Paper did not evolve to be money because it better satisfies most of the properties of money. There is only one monetary property where paper money particularly excels over gold. That property is portability.

There are two separate interest groups to consider when thinking about switching from gold to paper notes as currency—the government and the people.

Governments and central banks naturally prefer fiat money because it allows for more control over the currency supply. Manipulating a currency's supply can allow a well-run central bank to reduce the length of economic recessions and keep economic booms occurring longer. Yet as will be explored in the following chapters, a government-issued fiat currency has numerous, less obvious downsides as well, such as the destruction of individual savings, increased debt burdens, and rising inequality between the wealthy and the poor. Still, governments are happy to accept these trade-offs for the benefits that come with controlling the printing press.

For individuals, however, the benefit is not so clear. Accepting a fiat money society means sacrificing personal financial security for the supposed service of the greater societal good. If there had been a push to move directly from gold coins to fiat notes, there would have been pushback from the general public.

The only way for such a significant shift in how money worked to occur was for people not to realize that a change was happening at all. Paper money became popular when it represented actual gold held in vaults, which can be thought of as gold warehouses. People were comfortable trading paper notes that represented gold that they knew they could physically get at any time by bringing their paper notes to the redeeming institution.

As time went by and generations passed, children were raised that had never experienced anything other than paper notes. To them, the paper *was* the money, not gold. Fiat money was only possible because it was customary to use paper as money in the minds of people, even though the difference between a gold-backed note and a fiat note is significant. In the US, it took many years for this "evolution" to occur. The severing of America's psychological link to gold as money began when President Roosevelt made gold ownership illegal in 1933.

From 1971 onward, control of the supply of US dollars has firmly resided in the hands of the Federal Reserve. There is no longer any true limit to the number of dollars that can be created as there was under the gold standard. The only constraint on the dollar's supply is the vague notion of "discipline." Since the Federal Reserve operates on the dual mandate of low unemployment and controlling inflation, only under a fiat standard is the institution completely able to manipulate certain aspects of the economy to meet these goals.

The primary way that new money has been created in the US since the Federal Reserve's birth is through interest rate movements and debt issuance. When a person goes to the bank to take out a loan, new currency is created that did not exist before. By controlling the interest rates that banks use when giving loans to customers, the Federal Reserve can influence how much new currency is created for the economy. When interest rates are low, more money is made because the cost to repay the loans is relatively cheap. When rates are high, people are less likely to apply for loans because of the increased cost of paying them back. As a representative example, a person is more likely to borrow $100 if they need to repay $102 than if they need to repay $110.

To put it bluntly, this system makes the entire modern economy run. The impact cannot be understated. A system of money is the base layer on which a civilization is built. There is no society without money, and in fact, a society can be defined through its choice of money. Almost all economies today operate using a similar approach and, indeed, the global economy today takes on the defining characteristic of its money. The entire world runs on debt.

INFLATION

AFTER THE DOLLAR left the gold standard in 1971, the monetary procedure did not materially change overnight. While the cap on the number of dollars that could be created was lifted with the ending of Bretton Woods, it is not as though the Federal Reserve immediately went out and printed as much money as they wanted. Intelligent people work at the Fed, people who understand the risks that inflation can pose. Still, the absence of the restriction on money supply that the gold standard provided led to a consistent increase in the amount of new currency entering circulation. Inflation was a problem throughout the 1970s and continued throughout the early '80s, peaking at 13.5% in 1980.[42]

For the readers of this book who are in the beginning stages of understanding the importance of money, it is essential to understand just what an inflation percent of 13.5% means. Inflation, traditionally measured using the Consumer Price Index (CPI), represents the price of a basket of goods that most Americans need. The change in prices of this basket of goods over time is the official inflation rate statistic. It is a flawed measurement (to be discussed in more detail later) that is intended to gauge the rise in prices of goods, essentially measuring a currency's devaluation.

When inflation rose in 1980, it meant that the price of goods was 13.5% higher on January 1, 1981, than on January 1, 1980. The average cost of everything that people buy—food, electricity, toasters, etc.—rose by 14% in a year. High inflation means that your dollars buy fewer goods and services than they did the year before.

Imagine you have a savings account with $100 in it. A year with 14% inflation is equivalent to someone taking $14 out of your bank account, leaving you with only $86. Inflation is an invisible tax, one most people do not appreciate because it is hidden. Instead of seeing your bank account balance go down, you simply are not able to buy quite as much food as you did before. The outcome is the same both ways, however. Persistent high inflation is devastating to the savings of Americans through the destruction of their purchasing power.

The trend of rising inflation eventually subsided in the mid-1980s, yet the continued steady expansion of the money supply has continued uninterrupted. There is no longer the constant fear of inflation that existed in decades past, although keeping inflation low is still one of the Federal Reserve's two mandated goals. The reason inflation has stayed relatively low, even as the money supply has expanded, is because human productivity has dramatically increased over the last forty years.

As technology has continued to evolve and there is constant progress in developing new tools that improve efficiency, humans can create goods more effectively than ever. Put another way, the advancement of technology allows us to grow more food and manufacture more cars than ever. The improvement in skill and knowledge is deflationary, meaning it makes goods cheaper. This has the opposite effect of printing money—which is inflationary—and the two outcomes have primarily canceled each other out in recent history.

This juxtaposition, where the deflationary aspects of technology have hidden the most obvious effect of new money creation (inflation), has led our society to disassociate many of today's political debates, such as increasing wealth disparity, rising costs of healthcare, and inequality, from the creation of new money itself.

Nonetheless, the United States' economy has run relatively smoothly since the battle with inflation in the early 1980s. Productivity has continued to rise, on average quality of life has steadily improved, and there have been few severe economic downturns. By most standard metrics, the US economy has been in excellent shape.

DEBT

WITH THE MONEY supply steadily expanding since the United States left the gold standard, the level of debt within America has steadily grown. This mounting debt is part of the natural mechanism that the modern system of money incents because new money issuance essentially dilutes the value of every individual dollar. Since 1971, the supply of dollars circulating has expanded from around two trillion to over twenty trillion at the start of 2020. Debt has grown at both the national and individual levels. These two go hand in hand and can be seen through the steady drop in interest rates over the last forty years. In the early 1980s, the interest rate peaked at around 20%. Today, rates are near zero.[43]

Interest rates play a role in an economy in two ways—saving and borrowing. For savers, the interest rate is the return that a deposit will earn on savings in a bank. With the 20% interest rate of the early 1980s, for every $100 kept in the bank, a depositor would receive an additional $20 in interest payments every year. This is a massive return, as the average S&P 500 stock return is approximately 7% per year. Savers like high interest rates because it allows for the possibility to earn a risk-free yield on deposits. There is no worrying about market crashes or economic downturn. Your money is safe in the bank.

For borrowers, however, high interest rates are terrible. When interest rates are high, it is more costly to take out a loan. In the same high-rate environment of the early 1980s, if an individual borrowed $100 from the bank, they would eventually need to repay $120 to fulfill the loan.

Since our economy is based on debt, central banks and governments believe it is more important for borrowers to be happy than savers, evidenced by the steady drop in interest rate yields since 1980. Borrowing fuels growth and keeps the modern economy running. The reduced rates encourage more borrowing, more investment, and, *theoretically*, more growth. While there have been a few economic blips during this time, there have been few periods of outright economic depression.

However, what has happened is a steady progression of small problems that stem from the constant issuance of new currency and debt. These issues gradually grow larger over time, with consequences stretching throughout the entire economy. While these problems have been building for fifty years, it is the 2008 Great Recession that accelerated our monetary journey and set America—and the rest of the world—into the state of political unrest that exists today.

2008

I N 2008, THE global economy crashed with the onset of
what is now known as the Great Recession. Economies
across the world ground to a halt as the world experienced
the most significant financial crisis since the Great Depression in the 1930s.

While the recession itself began in 2008, the causes for
the downturn had been in place for a few years already as
investment assets such as mortgage-backed securities (MBS)
became more commonly issued and traded among financial
institutions.

THE MBS DEBACLE

ESSENTIALLY, AN MBS is a financial instrument whereby
a bank gives a buyer a loan to buy a home and then sells
that loan to an investment bank. The investment banks then
bundle many of these loans together and allow them to be
sold and traded in financial markets.

Throughout the early 2000s, banks became increasingly
willing to give out mortgage loans without performing due
diligence on prospective home buyers. Banks were giving
out substantial loans without adequately vetting that their
clients would be able to pay the loans back. The populariza-
tion of MBSs meant that banks could get cash right away
since they were selling the loans to financial institutions,
essentially taking the banks themselves off the hook for the

loan repayment. Tens of thousands of homes were purchased by new homeowners who were not earning enough income to repay the mortgages they now owed.

Investment banks had thought that they were protected from defaults through another financial derivative known as a "credit-default-swap," which was meant to be a form of insurance for this exact type of problem. The investment banks underestimated the size of the housing bubble, however. Eventually, homeowners started failing to repay their loans *en masse*. The severity of the problem was such that insurers did not have the capital to cover the credit-default-swap holders. The housing market crashed, and many financial institutions, such as AIG, Merrill Lynch, and Lehman Brothers, went bankrupt.

Now is the time to explain the difference between monetary and fiscal policy. Monetary policy is determined strictly by the Federal Reserve. The Fed aims to control the interest rates that banks set and the total supply of money circulating in the economy while also attempting to keep both inflation and unemployment in check. Fiscal policy, on the other hand, refers explicitly to legislation passed by Congress. This often requires the Fed to increase the money supply, though for specific reasons and programs. Congress is not intended to control how the US dollar as a system functions. As we continue to explore throughout the remainder of the book, however, we will find that the attitude around this is beginning to change.

THE GOVERNMENT'S RESPONSE

IN 2008 AND 2009, the two parts of the response to the Great Recession permanently altered the way the economy functions in the United States.

First was the Emergency Economic Stabilization Act of 2008 that was, in essence, a bank bailout to save many of the institutions that would have otherwise permanently gone out of business due to the recession. This action, which certainly lessened the economic harm that would have occurred had these businesses been allowed to fail, taught many companies the wrong lesson in the decade that followed the crisis. Instead of being a warning sign for what not to do, the bank bailout showed the world that the US government would not allow many of its largest companies to fail.

The second response to the Great Recession was the American Recovery and Reinvestment Act of 2009. This stimulus package, of about 800 billion dollars, was intended to revive the flailing economy. There had never been a stimulus of this size before, but with the bill's passage, the precedent was set for the future. Without the 2009 legislation, the stimulus passed in 2020 during the COVID-19 pandemic may never have happened, certainly not at its size. The events of 2008 set the stage and altered the course of the world's economic history.

With the 2008 crisis, the world began to adopt a form of monetary policy known as "quantitative easing" (QE). Quantitative easing is an unconventional policy that central banks had only employed on limited occasions in the past. QE refers to a situation when a central bank purchases securities available for sale in the open market, directly engaging in asset purchases. These purchases add liquidity to long-term securities markets.

Liquidity is one of the most important concepts to understand in financial markets. In short, liquidity represents the amount and ease with which an asset can be sold. Cash is the most liquid asset there is. If a person wants to get rid of their cash, they can find almost anybody willing to take it. Everybody takes cash. Equities on the stock market are highly liquid as well. A person looking to sell $10,000 of Apple stock will have no issue finding a buyer and will be able to liquidate their stock in exchange for cash almost instantly. High liquidity means that there is a significant quantity of buyers and sellers in a market.

On the other hand, real estate is an example of a relatively illiquid asset. Yes, it has value, but it is not easy to sell. You cannot sell your house on the same day that you decide you want to sell it. There are a limited number of prospective buyers looking for homes in your area who may be willing to pay your asking price.

In a recession, liquidity dries up in markets. Instead of a healthy market with tens of thousands of buyers and sellers, people get scared. Fearing that the economic downturn will continue, buyers abandon the marketplace, leaving only sellers. Phrased differently, large recessions create liquidity issues, where sellers cannot easily sell their assets since there are far fewer buyers.

Usually, people are less interested in borrowing money during recessions. When the stock market is falling and Americans are losing their jobs, the desire to take out loans for investment falls, since confidence in the economy is low. The Federal Reserve wants people to take out new loans, however, to stimulate the economy. To incentivize this, the Fed reduces interest rates which reduces the cost of borrowing.

Eventually, rates approach 0% and are unable to go any lower. This has traditionally been the limit of what the Federal Reserve can accomplish to stimulate the economy. If rates are 0% and people still do not want to borrow, the Fed is traditionally out of tools in their toolkit. At this point, any additional stimulus for the economy needs to be done through fiscal policy, leaving Congress to pass legislation that allows the money and programs to reach the economy.

With quantitative easing, central banks worldwide have a new tool added to their arsenal. Even when people and businesses are uninterested in borrowing, central banks can use QE to ensure that markets maintain enough liquidity to function. While initially intended to be a temporary measure, it is now a permanent fixture in financial markets, with the Fed regularly buying bonds on the open market to add liquidity.

With the COVID-19 pandemic in 2020, however, quantitative easing has morphed into something significantly more expansive. The amount of money created by the Federal Reserve has exploded. Both monetary and fiscal policies have reached a level of expansion that have not been seen before in the modern world. If a stimulus package can be $2 trillion, like the one in 2020, why should we stop there? Why not $3 or $4 trillion instead? We have all forgotten about the question that every seven-year-old asks, "Why can't we just print as much money as we want?" In this way, the decade since the 2008 recession accelerated the trends already occurring since the US left the gold standard in 1971.

The decade that has followed the American Recovery and Reinvestment Act of 2009 has been one where stimulus is constant. We cannot always see it, but it is there, operating in the background. And in the transition to an economy of never-ending stimulus, something significant happened.

The dollar broke.

PART II:
MODERN MONEY

PEOPLE DO NOT
UNDERSTAND MONEY

W E HAVE A system of money that encourages Americans to engage in behavior that is detrimental to their well-being. First and foremost, this starts with debt.

A BRIEF RECAP

THE PRIMARY WAY that new money is created in our modern money system is through debt issuance. When loans are given—to both individuals and businesses—new money is essentially created out of nowhere. When loans are paid back, the money is destroyed and is no longer in circulation.

While this has always been the primary way that new money is issued in America, there are notable differences between how money works now and how it used to work. Up until 1971, the United States was on a gold standard. A gold standard means that each dollar represented a certain backing of gold reserves. In essence, the dollar was simply a paper proxy for gold.

When President Nixon ended the gold standard in August 1971, life did not feel any different for the average American. They continued to be paid the way they always had been, and the prices of goods still reflected the dollar value that citizens had known before. Money had, in fact, changed, however.

For all intents and purposes, the dollar as we know it

ᵤ an entirely different currency than it was in 1971. ᵤany of the rules are the same, but now with no limits. While on a gold standard, there was a cap on the amount of new money that could be created. Since 1971, this is no longer the case. While most Americans may not be able to notice a difference, the impact of this difference—the lack of a cap on the money supply—cannot be overstated.

THE PIZZA ECONOMY

IT IS NECESSARY now to understand exactly why a society cannot merely create as much money as it wants. After all, if new money could help people, why would we not want to do that? To illustrate why, we will use two examples.

Take a look at the room around you right now as you read this. Imagine that the space represents an entire economy. There may be a desk, some chairs, a couch, cups, tables, etc. In this hypothetical economy, the total supply of money is $100, meaning that every item in the room right now has a price, and the sum of everything in the room equals $100. What happens if the supply of money for this room economy magically doubles to $200? What about the room changes? Nothing.

The reason nothing changes is that there is still the same amount of goods in the room now that there was before. There are the same number of chairs, couches, cups, and tables in an economy of $100 as there is in the economy of $200. What does change, however, is the price of the goods in that economy. There is still one table in the room, but where the table was worth $20 in an economy of $100, it is worth $40 in an economy of $200. An item's price in an economy is not determined only by the supply and demand dynamics of that item in isolation; the price is also affected by the total money supply circulating. Therefore, creating new currency does not add any new value to an economy. It simply changes the value of the goods.

What happens, then, when we hear of new money being created to fund something such as a new government program? What is happening in that case if printing more money does not buy more goods?

Think of America as a pizza pie cut into eight slices, with each slice representing a portion of the country's total money. When the government and the Federal Reserve print money, they are not making the pizza pie any larger. The same amount of goods remains the same—like steel, lumber, food, etc.—as before. Printing money divides the pizza into more slices—instead of eight slices of pizza, the pizza pie is cut into nine pieces, and that ninth slice is whatever the government decided to print the money for. Who is the loser in this scenario? It is the people who have the other slices of pizza. Before, they had one-eighth of the pie, and now they have one-ninth.

In real life, the other slices of pizza represent the savings of all Americans. If the money supply is increased by 10% to fund a new program, every American essentially has 10% of their purchasing power cut to create that ninth slice of pizza. This situation hurts Americans with lower incomes more than anyone else. While the wealthy also lose 10%, they are less affected because they have more slices of pizza to begin with. Americans with lower incomes cannot afford to have their purchasing power cut by 10%, so they are hurt the most. In a way, this is exactly like a flat tax on savings.

This concept can be challenging to comprehend and truly understand, especially for someone who has never thought about money in this systemic manner before. It is particularly difficult to grasp because the numbers in a citizen's bank account will not change when new money is created. If a person had $10,000 in the bank one day, they would still have $10,000 the next.

Additionally, prices do not magically change overnight due to an influx of new money creation. Not only does it take time for prices to adjust, often quite a while, but the rise in new prices is not always evenly distributed. The sector of the economy that has first access to the new money will likely see prices in that sector change more rapidly than in another sector. As we'll see in later chapters, costs have not been rising linearly over the past half-century. Instead of prices rising evenly, increasing costs have predominately hit certain sectors of the economy, such as healthcare and college tuition.

Every new dollar created lowers the value of every dollar already in existence. The pizza pie does not get bigger when new money is printed. Instead, the pie gets cut into smaller slices. At this point, it becomes necessary to understand the ramifications of the constant resizing of our pizza economy and examine further how this penalizes low-income earners and families.

CAN WE INCREASE OUR WEALTH?

THERE IS OFTEN no such thing as saving when you are a low-income earner. It is a necessity to spend your money. The days are spent working for a low wage, and that money then needs to be used on food, shelter, and other essential items. Many people and families often do not have enough money to grow their savings since almost everything earned needs to be spent. If there is leftover money, it may be saved or used for an emergency fund. Crucially, while there may be some money to save, there is likely not enough money to invest. This is not the case for the middle class and above.

Investments are, by their nature, somewhat risky. The reward for a good investment is paid for by the risk of the investment failing. To understand how our system of money hurts the poor, one must look at the role of general investing in the stock market.

Most investors in the stock market do not have a clue about stocks. They have no idea which companies are suitable investments and which are bad investments. For the most part, this is fine. Investing in the stock market has become quite simple. No longer does one have to go through a complicated process to own stocks. You can easily download an app on your phone and be buying stocks within five minutes.

The process of buying stocks was made even easier with the rise of index fund investing. When an investor buys an index fund, usually a mutual fund or an exchange traded fund (ETF), the investor chooses to own funds that track the entire stock market instead of buying select individual stocks. Instead of having a portfolio consisting of stocks like Amazon and Visa, an index fund lets investors own exposure to the entire stock market in one fund.

This makes investing much more straightforward. Families do not need to choose between conducting extensive individual research on companies or hiring professional advisors to make their investment choices for them. Now it is possible to simply invest in a fund where the only bet is that the stock market will go up over time. Without worrying about any individual company's performance, an investor can follow the market as a whole.

Index fund investing has become incredibly popular. These financial instruments have been available for many years, but have gained prominence over the last decade. Whereas in 2006, index fund investing accounted for less than 25% of the total stock market, it now accounts for nearly half of the stock market. The rise of index funds has now made it easier than ever to invest in the stock market and to do so in a way that exposes the investor to as little risk as possible.

But why is this relevant?

Prior to 1971, when the US was on the gold standard, there was a limit to the number of new dollars that could be created. Once the country left the gold standard, this cap was lifted. There could be as many new dollars as the Federal Reserve wanted, and they have certainly taken advantage of that ability. While less than two trillion dollars were circulating in 1970, there are now over 20 trillion dollars, an increase of ten times.

As mentioned earlier, everyday Americans did not feel the impact of all the new money circulating after the US left the gold standard. Life continued to feel the same. However, the reality is that the creation of all the new money that is now floating around has had disastrous effects on the poorest Americans.

The primary approach to new money creation in America is through loans within the traditional banking system. Over the last fifty years, the quantity of loans given out by the banks has skyrocketed, which has led to the tenfold growth in the money supply. There are two aspects of this process that disproportionately hurt Americans with lower incomes—access and purchasing power.

The first is a matter of access. Since new money is traditionally created through bank loans, it follows that the new money goes to those taking out the loans. In most cases, these people tend to earn incomes in the middle range or above. Americans with lower incomes have to spend their savings on necessities and are less likely to wager on the risk of taking out a new loan. When individuals have more wealth security, they are more willing to make riskier decisions to pursue a higher reward. At the same time, wealthier Americans are also taking out larger loans, which leads to a scenario where most of the new income created through bank loans goes directly to the upper class.

In addition to the fact that the majority of new money created is given directly to the already wealthy, the purchasing power of each dollar is falling over time. Remember, new money creation does not make the pizza any larger. While many people do not realize just how significantly their dollar is devaluing over time, they tend to understand that money needs to be invested instead of simply saved in bank accounts. Wealthier people understand this best, as they have the luxury of relative economic security.

THE WEALTH GAP

THE PROBLEM WITH this is that the poor get poorer and the rich get richer. The simple act of creating new money hurts the poor. Low-income workers already have minimal savings, because they need to spend the money they earn on necessities. Whatever they can save, they keep in cash savings in the bank. When new money is created by the Federal Reserve or by the government, these already low savings accounts lose purchasing power as slivers of their already small slices of the economic pizza are taken away.

Investing compounds this effect. Instead of saving money in the bank, wealthier people usually invest their money. They understand that they need their dollars to grow over time and they have the economic security to afford to have less liquid cash on hand. This is not the fault of the investors. They understand that if money is not growing, it is losing value. A dollar today is worth more than a dollar tomorrow. People may not always understand how stocks work or how to analyze the income statement of a company, but thanks to new tools making it easier than ever to invest, more people can participate in the markets.

The inevitable result of the way the modern monetary system works is that affluent Americans get to watch their wealth grow over time by investing in financial assets like stocks. Less wealthy Americans fall further behind as their already minimal cash savings increasingly loses purchasing power.

There is no way to avoid this result as long as the supply of new money increases. The effects are a direct consequence of money supply growth. While this has always been the case, the effects have not always been so extreme. The wealth gap between the rich and the poor has reached levels not seen since the Great Depression. During the period between 1929 and now, the wealth gap was much smaller. What changed?

The critical point at which wealth inequality began to grow again occurred when the United States left the gold standard in 1971. At this point, there was no longer any limit to the supply of new dollars that could be created, and the Federal Reserve did not hesitate to begin doing so. The amount of new money created has been so extreme that it has led to significant price growth in certain sectors of the economy and contributed heavily to the devaluation of the dollar's purchasing power.

Though many Americans have recognized the problems that have occurred over the last fifty years, they fail to diagnose the problems' actual source. Instead of blaming political factors—left versus right or capitalism versus socialism—one must go deeper and look at the money. The increase in the money supply has gradually caused growing cracks in our civilization's base layer—the system of money.

So, what happens from here?

ECONOMIC CYCLES

The MODERN SYSTEM of money has clear causes and effects that impact everyone, often negatively. If that is the case though, why is nothing done about it? The truth is that it is rare to think about money. For Americans, having the most stable and demanded currency on the planet is a luxury that no other country has. This privilege has resulted in ignorance about how money works and the effects it has on society.

ECONOMIC THEORIES

THE SYSTEM HAS conditioned us to think this way. The idea that saving is bad for an economy is taught in every economics class around the country. There are no differing schools of thought in economics anymore. Whereas in the previous century there was a regular battle between the monetarists and the Keynesians, this is no longer true. Now all sides believe in the same general approach to macroeconomics—increase spending and debt—though they differ significantly on how to wield that power. In this way, all modern economics falls on the same side of the proverbial coin. Instead of saving, debt is encouraged.

Take a look at this sentence. "I feel more secure when I save my money instead of investing it. I do not want to go into debt."

It is nearly universally agreed upon in modern economics

that the above statement is bad for an economy and should be discouraged. Yet after researching and understanding monetary history, the idea that saving is bad begins to make less sense. While debt growth can lead to economic growth, time and time again throughout history debt eventually becomes too large to manage and significant consequences ensue.

Prior to 1971, there was a limit to the amount of new money that could be created, which meant that there was a limit on how much debt could be created. The system worked well in this case. When constrained by a money supply cap, the Federal Reserve was, for the most part, successfully able to keep debt growth within reasonable limits, and the dollar thrived as a result. There were only a few times where credit and debt became too easy to obtain, such as prior to the Great Depression, when a significant bubble formed and eventually popped. There were also moments in which the constraint on the money supply was broken, as with World War I and World War II.

It is worth taking a moment to expound on the significance of the previous statement. Beginning with World War I, many countries across the globe suspended the link between their currencies and the precious metal to which they were pegged. These countries would not have been able to finance their war efforts if they had still been tied to a gold standard. This highlights the way that our modern fiat money system advances war.

With no limit to the supply of new money creation, conflicts can extend for as long as governments wish. There is no financial barrier within the currency itself that prevents perpetual war, which is how, in 2020, we can see things such as the perpetual presence of the US in the Middle East and the decade-plus war that occurred in Iraq. If there were a limit to the amount of new money that could be created, these wars would not have extended for so long.

There is a game theory element to this as well. While printing unlimited money hurts a country in the long run, it is undoubtedly helpful in the short term. For example, in the case of a world war, as soon as one country decides to create infinite money to fund a perpetual war, their opponent must do the same as well or risk being decimated in battle. This creates a negative feedback loop where all countries participating in a war become incentivized to abandon their currency restrictions, even though it hurts their money's stability and strength.

During the twentieth century, countries always tried to return to valuing their dollar at an exchange rate linked to a precious metal, though it was challenging to do. These countries would often try to reestablish the ratio of currency to gold used prior to the war, even though significant new money had been created. When this happened, the peg would inevitably break and need to be adjusted because, with the excess currency circulating, each unit of currency had lost value and would thus flow into scarce assets like gold. This makes it impossible for the exact exchange of gold to be returned to the ratio used when there were fewer units of money in circulation.

At present, the peg of the dollar to hard money is long gone. As a result, there are now wars that do not end, with conflicts that do not even feel like wars because Americans do not feel the need to pay attention. This is only possible because of the lack of a cap on the dollar supply. War can now be funded at will.

This approach to spending has led to a reliance on debt. Debt has always been a source of growth for the American economy. Loans are an essential tool for enabling access to capital for those who do not have it themselves. It is good for a certain amount of debt to be issued. The problems arise when the debt grows with no signs of stopping.

DEBT CYCLES

HISTORICALLY, ECONOMIES GO through what are known as "debt cycles." There are short-term debt cycles and long-term debt cycles. The cycles occur as credit is generally expanded over a period of time. Both debt and income grow, and the economy experiences a flourishing bull market with high growth. However, at a certain point, debt begins to grow faster than incomes, which results in difficulty paying back the loans. When this happens, there is a liquidation of assets to fund debt repayment, income falls further, and growth falls. This is a natural cycle.

Eventually, the economy hits the bottom of the cycle, meaning a recession, and credit begins to expand again, thus starting a new phase. Typically, short-term debt cycles occur every decade or so and tend to only result in mild recessions. The bottom of a short-term debt cycle is usually still a bit higher than before the run started, meaning that there is more cumulative debt at the end of a short-term cycle than at the beginning, even after a recession.

Long-term debt cycles are the accumulation of many short-term debt cycles. Since the bottom of each short-term debt cycle is higher than the last, the amount of debt in the economy grows over time. Long-term debt cycles function in the same way that short-term ones do, where credit and debt grow at an increasing pace. This is fine as long as income growth is rising faster than the increase in debt. Eventually, however, debt begins to outpace income growth. At this point, the debt becomes difficult to service. On average, every seventy to one hundred years, the economy's cumulative amount of debt reaches its apex point, the top of a long-term debt cycle.

By their nature, long-term debt cycles are much more severe than short-term cycles. As debt and credit grow over decades, the economy advances to a higher level than previously seen. Incomes soar, and prosperity is felt by most in the public. The issue is that, at some point, growth in the economy became fueled by debt. Where at first debt growth fueled income growth, the debt later inevitably outpaces income. It is unavoidable because when an economy is functioning smoothly and the public feels prosperous, people become more likely to take on more debt since they believe that the economy is performing well. Of course their debt will be paid off, right?

As an economy reaches the zenith point of the bull market, more investment and more debt are being continuously created due to sky-high consumer confidence. The result of this is that debts that would not be taken on by cooler-prevailing heads are taken on. There is an influx of bad investments. As debt growth outpaces income growth, it becomes increasingly difficult to service those debts. The bad debts will be the first to fail. A circular effect occurs where investments must be liquidated to pay off debts, which lowers the price of financial assets, making it harder to service debts, and so forth.

This is how the economic cycle works. It is not something that can be legislated away. When an economy performs well for a long enough time, debt always eventually outpaces income growth. Technically, it is the Federal Reserve's job, or the central bank of any country, to manage this. If the central bank sees that debt is increasing too quickly, they can raise interest rates to reduce investment. When interest rates are high, money in the form of loans is more expensive.

In long-term debt cycles, the effects of the trough (the low point in the curve) of the cycle are amplified. Since the debt has gradually been built up for multiple decades, it is not as simple as resetting the economy through a minor, mild recession. Instead, what typically ends up materializing is a much larger depression.

When more significant recessions and depressions occur, central banks and governments often step in to provide assistance to both markets and citizens. Assistance can be given in a few different ways, but the most common is through money printing and various forms of stimulus.

ADAPTING TO DEBT

IT IS IMPORTANT to note that the effects of downswings in an economy are naturally deflationary. Paying off debt means that a person spends less on themselves in order to pay down the debt, resulting in less economic spending than there would otherwise be. Since personal consumption is reduced, demand for goods and services falls, which lowers prices. Financial assets are sold off to pay debts as well, compounding the deflationary effects further. Deflation means that the real value of the debt grows over time. As prices of goods, services, and assets fall, the amount of debt owed stays the same, meaning that each dollar spent while paying off debt could otherwise have been used to purchase increasingly more goods.

This is important because a deflationary environment allows the government to enact stimulus without causing rampant inflation. Stimulus and money printing, which are inflationary, negate some of the deflationary effects in a downturned economy. Due to this delicate balance, the degree of stimulus requires a careful balance by central banks and governments. It is difficult to find the right mix of stimuli to counter a deep recession. If too much money printing is done, there is the risk of high consumer price growth through inflation.

The best way to manage a depression is up for debate. There have been many times throughout history where a central bank has shortened depressions through various forms of stimulus. There have also been many cases where central bank intervention has made matters significantly worse. It is not easy to manage a depression.

There is a problem, though. Today is not the past. In previous times in the United States, debt was able to skyrocket at various points in history, but not to the degree that it has today. During the Great Depression, the ratio of public debt to GDP reached approximately 40%. By the end of 2019, that ratio was 106%.[44] Outside of wartime, this level of debt is unprecedented in the United States.

Clearly, there is a lot of debt, but what does it mean? And how did it get this way? It means that our economy has increasingly become reliant on debt, which can be directly traced back to leaving the gold standard in 1971. At that point, when there was no longer a cap on the money supply, there could be as many dollars circulating as the Federal Reserve wanted, which also meant that there could be an infinite amount of new debt that could be created.

As stated before, there are more than ten times the US dollars circulating in 2020 as there were in 1971, from about $2 trillion to $20 trillion (prior to the COVID-19 stimulus).[45] While interest rates peaked in 1980, they have been steadily declining since then and are now essentially 0%.[46] As the rate has fallen, more money has been created in the form of new debt being taken out. Lower interest rates encourage debt by reducing the price of money—the cost to take out a loan—while at the same time reducing the benefit that savers get from keeping their money in the bank.

The lowering of interest rates, combined with removing a money supply ceiling, *a la* the gold standard, has led the country to a position where it now cannot survive without debt. If the debt total was a snowball rolling down the side of the mountain, the US is only halfway down, and the snowball has turned into an avalanche.

As the money supply and debt totals have continued to grow, individuals, companies, and governments have adapted to this economic environment. It has become second nature for individuals and companies to have as little cash on hand as possible. While many people may not understand the complexities of how the monetary system works, they often fully appreciate the need to invest in growing their money over time. Corporations act in similar ways. Only a few companies keep significant amounts of cash on hand, while most invest their money to avoid the melting-ice-cube effect, where dollars kept in a bank account lose value every year from inflation.

So much new money has been created, yet there is so little cash on hand. This is the crux of the debt problem, and it is a vicious circle. As more money gets created by the government and the Federal Reserve, there is an ever-increasing incentive to spend money instead of saving it. Since most new money is created through debt issuance, this effect is compounded further as money issued through debt is always spent and is never simply stored in a savings account.

The economy has grown completely reliant on debt in a way that has never happened before. So much new debt has been issued over the last fifty years that there is no way to unwind it. The scale of the debt has grown so massively that it is incomparable to previous points in American history, save for World War II. Active warfare is the only time that Americans have held this much debt, yet now the debt functions as part of our everyday lives. Unlike with WWII, there is no endpoint—the end of the war—at which point the monetary system will get back to normal. This is the new normal now, and there is no coming back from it.

The reliance on debt for an economy results in a self-reinforcing feedback loop. As the amount of debt grows continually larger, it requires more and more payment to feed the debt. In the past, when the growing amount of debt began to outpace growth in income, the economy would see the end of a short-term debt cycle and have a mild recession. This does not happen anymore. Instead of allowing the economy to reset itself, the policymakers in charge of the dollar have continued to reduce the price of money, attempting to keep cycles going for longer periods of time.

In a way, the debt cycles in the economy are akin to the workings of the development of forest fires. It is not wise for firefighters to put out every small fire that develops in the forest. Forest fires serve a purpose. They clean out the accumulating brush and undergrowth that develops in the forest over time. If every small forest fire is put out by firefighters, the brush continues to accumulate at the bottom of the forest floor. Eventually, this growth reaches a point where the fire that erupts is significantly more massive and is impossible to contain due to the lack of smaller fires before it.

The economy has become the same way. There are no small forest fires anymore. Policymakers do not allow for any minor blips in the economy to happen. Every forest fire is put out. This is dangerous. Economic downturns are natural. They allow for the economy to clear itself of bad investment.

Poorly run companies fail, and new, better companies grow from the ashes. It is the natural order of economic cycles, and it is healthy for the economy. An economy is not supposed to be good all the time.

We crystallized our future in 2008. During the Great Recession, as discussed in an earlier chapter, the housing price bubble in America popped. Like many recessions before it, the cause was bad debt. The American economy crashed.

Normally when a crash like this occurs, many companies will fail. Debt will be restructured. Poorly managed businesses disappear, and new ones arise in the aftermath. That is not what happened in 2008, however, and it changed the path of the American economy in a way that cannot be undone.

Instead of allowing the companies that caused the economic downturn to fail, it was determined that a financial bailout was needed to prevent the companies from going under. If these companies were allowed to fail, too many jobs would have been lost, and the economy would have suffered further. Thus, it was determined that a large stimulus must be passed, and the American Recovery and Reinvestment Act of 2009 was signed into law in February 2009.

There is no doubt that the stimulus package of nearly $800 billion reduced unemployment and lessened the duration of the recession. That fact is what makes economic analysis so difficult at times. It is easy to see that stimulus during a recession makes the recession less serious and less harmful to many citizens. The problem, which is exceedingly difficult for many to understand, is that this is not necessarily a good thing.

As previously noted, a recession at the end of a debt cycle gives the economy a chance to reset. When asset bubbles are caused by too much debt, specifically debt that resulted from malinvestment derived from the easy money that comes with low-interest rates, the lenders that allowed the bad debt to be issued are at fault. They were bad lenders. Instead of allowing these companies to fail from their poor business management, they were instead allowed to keep operating.

By bailing out these businesses, the economy never reset. The harmful brush that was supposed to clear out with the forest fire of the recession was not burnt away; it remained. In fact, it became worse.

WHY SOME PRICES RISE MORE THAN OTHERS

S OME PRICES RISE more than others. Over time, and particularly over the last fifty years, there has been a relevant divergence in the movement of prices. While many goods and services have remained relatively affordable for most Americans—although significantly devalued from their 1970's counterparts due to inflation—the cost of other goods has become increasingly expensive and unaffordable. Remarkably, these goods that have seen their prices rise the most are the goods that are considered the most necessary, important, and unavoidable expenses. These goods that have seen significant price inflation most notably include healthcare and college tuition.

That these sectors of the economy have seen their cost rise so much has been a common topic in political conversations. As healthcare has become increasingly unaffordable, it is the poor and the uninsured who suffer the most. The cost of college tuition has followed suit, which has led to millions of Americans taking on debt that becomes a severe burden to pay back later in life. At the same time, these struggling Americans look at the size of the stock market, which has been hitting all-time highs, increasing its participants' wealth, and it causes anger in them. How can it be that the poorest Americans cannot afford to pay for certain costs while the wealthy get wealthier from a stock market that keeps going up? Why is that fair?

ASK THE RIGHT QUESTIONS

THERE IS A crucial factor that is overlooked in these discussions, however. It is rarely asked *why* the cost of these goods and services has been rising so significantly, while others have stayed affordable. The reason behind the cost increases is often overlooked entirely, even though it should be the entire discussion. Instead, the "why" is ignored, and, rather, the blame is placed within whichever political narrative that individual subscribes to. If they believe that the wealthy are the root cause of suffering for less advantaged Americans, they will blame the rich. If they think it is an over-regulated market, they will blame the government.

All of this misses the point entirely, which is why these issues are unlikely to be fixed. The real question to be answered is, "Why are specific sectors of the economy experiencing such disproportional price growth in the first place?" The answer lies in the US dollar itself. In fact, the reason that the cost of healthcare is rising is the same reason that the stock market keeps hitting all-time highs.

As discussed earlier in this book, the creation of new money naturally leads to prices rising over time. This is because there is more money circulating for the same amount of goods. The price of goods and services is determined by a function of both the value of the goods compared to other goods and the total money supply circulating. An apple that costs $3 in a world where there are $1 trillion in existence becomes worth $6 in a world where there is now $2 trillion.

Throughout the last half-century, the supply of dollars

has been increasing exponentially, reaching a pinnacle with the COVID-19 pandemic. There are more than ten times the number of dollar bills than there were fifty years ago. Since it is the simple creation of new money that results in prices rising, then by the logic presented above, should the prices of all goods not have increased equally? Clearly, this has not been the case. Instead, the prices of many goods have remained low, while a few goods and services, many of which are highly demanded by and important to all, have experienced skyrocketing price growth.

When this topic is discussed, the focus is typically on the sectors of the economy where prices have become unaffordable for most Americans, such as healthcare, college tuition, and housing/real estate. It is natural and understandable for the attention to be drawn to these big-ticket areas of the economy. These goods and services represent things that almost everybody needs, in some shape or fashion. Looking at these areas is the wrong way to understand this problem, however. To properly comprehend this phenomenon occurring in the economy, we should instead focus our attention on the cheap goods. To understand why certain goods have gotten so expensive, we much first recognize why so many items have remained cheap.

TECHNOLOGY

OVER THE LAST seventy-five years, technology has been developing exponentially. Faster than most people can imagine. Humans do not intuitively understand the scope of exponential growth. While in reality, a piece of paper can only be folded seven times, think about the following question: how tall would a piece of paper be if you folded it in half fifty times? Paper is so thin that the answer could not be very significant, right? Perhaps the paper is a foot thick, maybe two? Not so. Exponential growth is massive, and repeatedly doubling the thickness of something even as thin as a sheet of paper produces extreme growth. If you folded a piece of paper fifty times, the stacked height would be tall enough to reach the sun.[47]

That is how significant exponential growth is, and it is relevant because technology has been improving at a rate that has never been seen before in history. In 1965, Gordon Moore predicted that the number of transistors that could fit on a microchip would double about every two years, essentially saying that technology's efficiency will effectively double every two years. This principle later became known as Moore's law. Continuing the paper example, technology is folding in half every two years. This law has proved primarily true and has led to a staggering improvement in technological development and efficiency, which most humans understand on the surface but fail to recognize the scope and significance of.

This growth has changed human life massively, mainly for the better. Through technology, we can create abundance. Technology allows us to create more goods in the same amount of time with less effort, making goods cheaper. It has never been less costly to produce essentially every item you may see when you look around the room you are in right now. We can manufacture more electronics and grow more food than ever before. This increasing abundance is why technological growth, which is essentially productivity growth, is deflationary. Since we can create more for less, prices naturally fall over time as there is no supply restriction to meet demand. Rapid growth in technology has affected many areas of the economy and has kept the costs down of almost all manufactured goods as production gets more efficient.

Industries that have seen their costs rise significantly throughout the previous decades tend to have one thing in common—technology does not create abundance in their field. While it may be true that, for example, an X-ray machine might be cheaper than it used to be, the field of medicine as a whole is not. This is because medicine is a constantly evolving field where innovations are researched and implemented daily. New techniques, new equipment, and new drugs to test are invented every year, and these things are costly.

While technology makes manufacturing cheaper over time, new machines and innovations will always be expensive, as there are limited parts, researchers, and manufacturers to create these new tools. These new inventions do not benefit from the abundance caused by technology in the same way that the food industry is helped. Now it is possible to easily grow more corn than ever before, to the point that more corn is produced than is needed by the people. This makes corn cheap.

In this same vein, the cost of college tuition also does not experience growth through technological progress. Technology makes teaching cheaper to a degree, with school supplies being reasonably inexpensive, but this does not translate to going to college itself. As with healthcare, the principal reason for this is the rise in the money supply combined with minimal technological improvement. It is now easier than ever for students to be able to attend college.

With the increase of the federal student loan program, students who did not previously have access to private financing for college could now take out loans to attend university. Because of this, more students began applying to schools. Think about this in the context of a food example. Due to technology, we have grown more corn to the point where supply has managed to meet and then exceed demand, which has kept prices low. This does not happen in education. Technology cannot create more schools. What determines the number of colleges in the country primarily has to do with regulation and barriers to entry. Since the supply of schools does not scale alongside the demand for schooling, prices rise.

Technology is the key takeaway here. In sectors of the economy where prices have remained comparatively low, massive productivity growth has occurred over the last half-century due to technological improvements. It is logical and makes sense that healthcare and college tuition are as expensive as they are. It should be expected, strictly from the dollar's devaluation that has occurred from excess currency supply inflation. It is normal for prices to skyrocket when this much new money is printed. The only reason so much of the economy has *not* experienced these price increases is that the growth of efficiency has been so exponential that its deflationary effects have been able to counter the inflationary effects from money printing.

Technology does not create abundance in every industry, however, which is critical to understand as the upcoming decade progresses. While the amount of new money circulating now compared to fifty years ago is extreme—more than tenfold—money printing as a political tool is just getting started. Whereas in the past, there was the notion that it is essential to be careful when it comes to spending, stimulus, and deficits, that concept has been completely abandoned. Republicans, who claim to be the "fiscally conservative" party, have significantly increased deficits in each of the party's previous two presidencies. Following suit,

Democrats have completely abandoned any semblance of monetary caution.

It makes sense why this has happened. If the dollars being printed are used to help a group of people, why would the government not do whatever it could to help? Unfortunately, this way of thinking represents a misunderstanding of how money works as a tool and how money systems rise and fall.

MINDSETS ARE SHIFTING

WITH COVID, THERE is a clear misconception as to the cause and effects of the stimulus packages that have passed. Many have cried about how it is unfair that Main Street is undoubtedly suffering due to the pandemic. Simultaneously, large companies, particularly the big four tech companies (Microsoft, Amazon, Apple, and Facebook) have seen their stocks soar. Why should the rich get richer while the poor suffer?

What is missing is a proper understanding of how money functions and how money naturally flows through an economy. It is the stimulus itself that has caused the appreciation in technology stocks. The more stimulus that is enacted, the more that inequality grows.

The mindset of the public is shifting to favor increased spending as well. Once considered to be laughable and extreme, policies such as universal basic income have now entered the political lexicon. While the bailout package for the 2008 Great Recession was less than $1 trillion, the first COVID-19 stimulus in the US was north of $2 trillion. The numbers are getting larger, and the public is becoming increasingly restless for more.

There will be no end to monetary stimulus. It is no longer

possible for governments and central banks to roll back their policies. Too much debt and government dependence have already been created, to the point that any attempt to put the brakes on expansionary monetary policy would result in an economic collapse.

It can be argued that letting the economy fail would be the proper approach. An economy is not supposed to require constant stimulus to stay afloat. That is a sign of a broken economy. The only way that a broken economy can be fixed is by allowing the businesses that are failing to fail. However, this option will never come about since it is politically unpalatable for an elected official to justify the loss of jobs and reduction of incomes that come with a recession. As a result, prices will continue to rise, particularly in those goods that benefit the least from technology development and scale.

Part of the issue is that the modern money system does not allow for prices to go down. It may seem counterintuitive, but it is said that prices must rise to ensure growth and continued innovation.

Due to a lackadaisical approach to monetary policy by central banks, monetary supply expansion is occurring at a rate not seen in the US since the American Revolution. With more than ten times the number of dollars circulating than there were just fifty years ago, it is a surprise to many that the overall official inflation statistic, the Consumer Price Index (CPI), has been below the targeted rate of 2% many years in the past decade. Central bankers are doing all they can to promote price inflation—through debasement of the currency—yet prices will not rise. Technological growth has been exponential, and therefore extremely deflationary, even to the degree that the prices of the majority of goods and services simply do not want to rise. Technological improvement has outpaced money printing.

This presents problems for government's central bankers. Debt has been rising exponentially, and a primary point of inflationary money is to relieve some of the debt burden by making debt worth less in real terms over time. As debt continues to grow rapidly, debt levels are at a point where the obligations are difficult, if not outright impossible, to pay off. Due to this, inflation is necessary as the only means by which the unbearable burden of amassed debt can be relieved.

Not only that, more and more inflation is needed over time as debt grows ever larger. But inflation numbers are low. Too low for central bankers. The US Federal Reserve announced in August 2020 that they are changing their inflation guidelines. Instead of aiming for a 2% inflation target per year, now the Fed will aim for a 2% average inflation over time. This is a key distinction, as it means that the Federal Reserve will allow inflation to go over 2% to counterbalance years where it is below 2%. The Fed has realized what most average Americans have not. The massive accumulation of debt can never be paid back in real terms. It has simply grown too large. The only solution they see is to inflate away the debt's real value by lessening the value of the dollar.

A SYSTEM FROM ANOTHER TIME

THE PROBLEM HERE is that our system of money was designed for another era. When the modern system of money came to be, new money creation affected prices more evenly. Mass production of items was limited. When new money entered the economy, technology could not heavily favor some industries over others to the extent that happens today. It is not that technological improvement has been uneven; on the contrary, most industries have seen significant advancements in cost and production efficiency from technology.

The issue arises when the industries that have not seen those benefits are the industries that are necessary for nearly every person. Someone cannot choose not to get sick. When they become ill or injured, they are reduced to financial ruin in a system designed to have prices keep going up.

It is the natural order of markets that—*sans* manipulation—prices will go down over time. This is because all human processes become more efficient as time goes by. As we refine our methods, create more goods, and continue to evolve intellectually, we can build more in less time for less cost. Costs going down is what would happen in a system that was left to function naturally. Prices rising over time is a human-made invention, not the natural order. Yet, the idea of inflation is never questioned. It is taken as a fact that inflation and the destruction of savings are necessary for an economy. This results from a society that takes money for granted, believing that the modern system of money will always work because it is all that they have known.

Due to all the accumulated debt, inflation is indeed necessary for the system as designed to function. The debt has reached levels so high that there are very few options available for handling it. Printing the money at all once to pay the debt is unfeasible because it would destroy the dollar's value in a heartbeat. The financially responsible thing to do would be to reduce government spending and raise taxes to run surpluses to reduce the debt. While this happened in the 1990s in the US, it is unlikely to ever happen again due to the sheer scale of the debt and deficit spending that has occurred since then.

There is no political incentive to do this either. As a thought experiment, given the massive annual deficit the budget has had every year since the early 2000s, consider the following: what would happen if a politician proposed a 1% budget cut for next year, with every single department in the government losing 1% of its funding? That proposal would be dead on arrival with no chance of passing and would be highly unpopular.

Democrats would be against the budget cut, claiming that it would take away essential services from those who need them. Republicans would be unwilling to accept cuts in many areas of the budget, such as the military. Both sides would shift to declaring that certain projects must be kept at the same funding level while pointing towards the other party's priorities as being the necessary place to cut.

Yet the debt does exist, and it is significant in size. The problem is that the modern monetary system provides zero short-term incentive for fiscal responsibility. It is easy to understand how this happens. Deficits do not feel real to most people because most people are not thinking about how systems of money actually function. When a 1% cut across all levels of government is proposed, all we see are the people who will suffer as a result of that department losing funding. What remains equally valid, but is less visible, are the long-term effects. The deficit spending is being paid for through a tax on everyone's savings through inflation, which overwhelmingly hurts the poor instead of the wealthy.

When designing any system, it is vital to consider the incentive structure put in place. The entire US dollar currency is managed primarily by a small group of unelected officials who operate behind closed doors, alongside a government that is increasingly comfortable using its power to deficit spend. The single restraint keeping the currency in check is the vague idea of responsibility by those in charge. However, throughout history, the urge to spend grows over time until finally any semblance of restraint is gone. When that happens, the currency suffers—as do its users. Whoever can print money will. Always.

Part of the issue is that our modern system is incapable of functioning without inflation, let alone if actual deflation were to occur. Modern money is, in fact, hardly modern at all. Recall the fall of the Roman Empire, and the devaluation of the denarius that occurred alongside it. When we create new dollars today, it is the same thing as when the Romans lowered the silver content in the denarius from 100% to 90%. In both cases, the currency loses value. It is just easier to see in the case of the Romans. Fundamentally, however, the result is the same.

Even so, as long as the monetary base was previously constrained by the total amount of precious metals held by the central bank, there was a limit to how much paper money could be printed. While this was ignored and abused in many nations, leading to hyperinflation, the more responsible countries such as the US, UK, and Switzerland were comparatively more limited in their monetary expansion.

Since 1971, this is no longer the case in the US, and the economy has evolved alongside the rising money supply. An increased money supply and ease of access to loans necessarily increases debt burdens, precisely what has happened in the country today. If deflation occurred, which again is the natural order of prices, the debt burden would be impossible to bear, and the economy would collapse. As such, the central bank knows that the only way to alleviate the debt burden is to aim for higher inflation.

The problem is that deflation is coming, and there is nothing that anyone can do to stop it. Technology is becoming ever more efficient and will create increasing abundance in many sectors as the decades pass. Given that technology's deflationary progression has already been able to counter the inflationary aspects of monetary printing, it is very possible that the larger deflationary forces will become significantly stronger than inflationary ones as technology grows even more powerful. Most people do not recognize this, however—even central banks.

When Jerome Powell of the Federal Reserve declared that the Fed will allow higher inflation, it was a declaration of war against falling prices. The Fed will not be able to win a war against technology, however. Where the inflation will be seen is in the economic sectors that do not benefit from technology. Inflation no longer means relatively equal price growth throughout the economy. Food might stay cheap, but your healthcare bill will keep going up.

A DEBT-BASED ECONOMY

T HE REASON OUR economy relies on debt is because of the inflationary monetary system on which the economy is based. When the Federal Reserve or the government creates new money, they effectively reduce the value of the money that is already circulating. Over time, this results in prices rising since the value of the dollar lessens.

Fundamentally, it is the creation of new money that primarily drives inflation, which therefore drives debt levels. By printing such a large amount of new currency over the last fifty years, the Fed is now encouraging people to invest their money and go into debt more than ever before. The economy has adapted to this in turn. Since it is impossible to store wealth in dollars, everyone is spending their money. They are investing in financial markets, and they are taking on debt. It has reached a point where now the economy needs more debt to survive. Over the last fifty years, particularly the last twenty, the amount of new debt accumulated has increased exponentially.

This system also benefits governments by allowing them to engage in spending that does not have to be paid for with taxes. It was not like this initially, but the government is now entirely reliant on inflationary money to fund itself. There has not been a budget surplus—meaning tax revenue exceeds government spending—since 2001, and it is unlikely that there will ever be one again. This is because the amount of taxes that would need to be raised to compensate for all the spending is so enormous that it would be political suicide to attempt. Either taxes would need to be massively increased, to the point where just taxing the rich would not be nearly sufficient, or the federal budget would need to be cut by over a third.

Another example for how holding cash has been disincentivized through the modern system of money can be seen with the increasing frequency in which corporations buy back their own stock.

COMPANY BUYBACKS

A STOCK BUYBACK, also known as a "share repurchase," occurs when a company buys back its shares from the marketplace with the cash that it has accumulated. A buyback is a way for a company to reinvest in itself. In order to conduct a buyback, a company must be profitable, resulting in excess cash, also known as "retained earnings." Typically, when a company has a significant amount of retained earnings, they do one of three things.

1. Use that money to invest in the company. This could include purchasing more equipment or machines, hiring more staff, expanding a research division, or many other possibilities to grow the business.

2. The second possibility is to spend a portion of excess reserves on a dividend to all the company shareholders. This allows all shareholders who are directly invested in the company to receive a portion of its profits. Often, companies will issue a fixed dividend based on the percentage of profits. For example, a company might have a policy that 3% of annual net income will be issued as a dividend.

Sometimes, however, there are simply no suitable means

to invest within a company further. It may already be operating efficiently, at peak margins, with satisfied shareholders. That is when companies might decide to choose option number three.

3. Buy back their own stock.

Saved money—accumulated retained earnings—does not always need to be immediately spent on the company itself, yet the company does not necessarily want to issue a dividend because they want to keep the cash on hand. Traditionally, this is where companies will hold ample cash reserves.

Many of these businesses understand how the modern system of money works, however. Holding a significant amount of cash in reserve is akin to holding a melting ice cube. Due to the exponential monetary supply expansion occurring for the last fifty years—and becoming increasingly pronounced over the last decade—large cash reserves are essentially melting, where their purchasing power becomes less and less each year. While Consumer Price Index (CPI) inflation has remained low, we have already discussed the mechanics of how the new money that is being created tends to find its way into financial assets. The opportunity cost of holding cash is that it becomes more expensive to purchase equities in the future as the dollar further devalues.

Therefore, many companies are aware that holding too much cash in reserves is a losing proposition. Still, there are not always good opportunities to invest within the company itself. They may also not find the prospect of investing in traditional funds and equities particularly appealing, perhaps because they see the general market as overvalued or for other reasons.

Buying back their own stock allows a corporation to keep its cash within the company while still benefiting from the appreciation in financial assets that modern money causes. Even further, stock buybacks result in increased control over the company's shares as they accumulate a higher and higher percentage of the total shares outstanding. By using excess reserves to repurchase company stock, the stock price may increase even further because the company is buying many of the available shares for sale. If there is more buying in a market than selling, an item's price will go up.

The sum of all the above factors is why stock buybacks have been occurring at an increasing speed over the last decade. As the money supply grows at a high rate, holding cash is becoming progressively further penalized. Rather than allowing their melting ice cube of cash reserves to lose more and more purchasing power, public businesses have chosen to buy back their stock.

While buying back stock can be a savvy way to use cash, there are ways in which it can end up a disaster. Recently, as the problems with modern money have become increasingly exacerbated, more stock buybacks have been occurring, with some businesses even going as far as to use almost the entirety of their cash to engage in share repurchases.

This works well when the economy is booming but can be catastrophic when a downturn occurs. By using a high percentage of their cash reserves to repurchase stock, a business may not have enough cash on hand in a time of recession. Since recessions result in falling stock prices and significantly reduced liquidity, making it more challenging to sell significant shares without crashing the price, businesses become trapped in their falling stock, with the only option being to sell for a considerable loss.

It is financial malpractice for a profitable business not to withstand an economic downturn, due to excessive share repurchases. Yet this is a trend that has been transpiring with increasing frequency in recent years. The most high-profile, recent case is Boeing's bankruptcy in March 2020—a profitable company every year.

GOVERNMENT BAILOUTS

ALONGSIDE THE POPULARITY of stock buybacks is the belief that the government should bail out important failing businesses to allow them to live to see another day. Following the 2008 recession, both large banks and the auto industry were bailed out, being deemed too big to fail. If these institutions failed, the reasoning went, the effects on the economy would be even worse. This has set a precedent and let large businesses know that they will be saved if they fail. The resulting effect is a moral hazard, where companies may engage in riskier behavior, knowing that they will likely be bailed out if needed.

All this has led to is a society that is both incredibly fragile and that has become entirely reliant on debt. There is nearly thirty trillion dollars' worth of debt in the United States today, and that number is growing rapidly. Constant new currency creation and the steady lowering of interest rates has shown market participants that keeping reserves in cash is bad business.

The problem is that there is no way to roll back all of this debt. It is a product of the system of money itself, particularly over the last fifty years. Individuals, businesses, and governments all have more debt than ever before. Since the debt amount is growing faster than incomes are growing, the debt is getting harder and harder to pay off. As a result, the Federal Reserve only has two choices.

Choice one is to stop printing money. If this happened, not only would there not be inflation, but deflation would occur as technology continued to make goods cheaper to produce. Deflation is terrible for people who are in debt because it increases the burden of that debt. If the government and the Federal Reserve allowed deflation to occur, debts would be defaulted on, banks would fail, and there would be a massive deflationary depression that could be more severe than even the Great Depression. This choice is an unacceptable outcome to most governments and central bankers.

Instead, they will take the opposite approach, operating under the belief that the only way to pay off the debt is to make the debt worth less by devaluing the currency. By choosing to avoid the actual cause of the debt problem, the Fed and the government will kick the proverbial can down the road. In turn, this will create an economy that is even more reliant on debt, higher income inequality, and increasingly distorted prices than it is right now. This approach is likely not sustainable, but it has indeed prevented a debt depression so far.

Thus, the way forward is a choice between two bad outcomes for the economy—fix the problem and suffer the depression that follows or push the issue off into the future as long as possible. The choice has already been made, and the latter path will be followed.

THE VALUE OF GOLD

A T FIRST GLANCE, gold does not have much of a place in the digital age. To the vast majority of people, gold is only a relic of ancient times, a shiny metal that we dig out of the ground. We know that gold has been around for a long time, and we know that it was valuable, but we do not know exactly *why* it has value except for some vague notions about being rare. Since we are an *evolved* technological species now, gold does not serve much of a purpose. It is ancient, obsolete, and only suitable for jewelry as a reminder of what was once truly valuable. Why would anybody possibly want to own gold for any other purpose besides being jewelry in 2021?

As it turns out, there are quite a few reasons why gold remains valuable. Now that we have had a chance to look in detail at some of the problems that the modern system of money has, it is worth taking the time to go backward and understand precisely why gold became the dominant monetary good before fiat money. Understanding the inherent flaws in fiat money is a necessary backdrop to understanding what has led gold and silver to be the metals that have ascended to the top of money's historical hierarchy.

It is not that using fiat money is necessarily better or worse than using gold. The concept to understand is that there are trade-offs with any monetary system, and the average American does not know that these concessions exist. Instead, they go about their days without ever thinking about how money fundamentally works and what its purpose is—which is to measure value and transfer it through both space and time. Modern fiat money improves on gold in the transfer of value through space, but the trade-off is that modern money is inferior at holding value through time.

GOLD'S LONG HISTORY

GOLD HAS A history that dates back an extremely long time. The first evidence of gold being stored is from 40,000 BCE in Paleolithic caves, far earlier than the first proper forms of money that developed around 9000 BCE.[48] As money, though, it was not until the ancient Egyptians where there is clear evidence of a major society definitively valuing gold. The Egyptians believed gold was the flesh of the sun god Ra. Prized by society, artisans made amulets, death masks, and other jewelry from gold.

In 1923, King Tutankhamun's burial chamber was discovered. When archaeologists opened the innermost of the three coffins, they found a golden death mask weighing twenty-two pounds.[49] The point here is that the history of gold is long. Gold has been valued for over 5,000 years. While many coins and forms of money have come and gone throughout the years, gold has always maintained its value. This should not be discounted, even now, when society can transport payments digitally with a few taps on their phones.

While many dismiss gold outright as an outdated monetary technology, this criticism comes without much meaning. In order to dismiss gold, one must be capable of describing why it was valuable in the first place and why that characteristic would not remain true today. Gold has been valuable longer than any other monetary good in history due to its scarcity. Remember, the most significant factor throughout monetary history that has determined whether a currency succeeded or failed has been its ability to store value. Holding value over time allows a society to worry less about day-to-day survival and allowed humans to spend more time on the technological innovations that began to occur around the dawn of Mesopotamia.

RARITY VERSUS SCARCITY

To CLEAR UP a common misconception, let us discuss rarity and scarcity and the importance of the difference in money. Rarity is the degree to which a good exists in limited quantity in absolute form, while scarcity refers to how difficult it is to increase the supply. The difference in the two definitions might seem slight, but the effects on whether money maintains its value over time are considerable.

You have likely heard of platinum already, but other metals such as palladium and rhodium are sometimes touted as "the next big thing" in precious metals. It is often mentioned that they are rarer than gold. This is true, but that does not mean they are more valuable. Rarity and scarcity are not the same thing. Because humans have been mining gold for so long, it is very difficult to increase the supply by more than 2% per year.

While these other metals may technically be rarer, we have not been mining them nearly as long. As such, the percent of supply that we can newly mine each year is much higher than gold. While there is less of them in the earth's crust overall, the supply inflation can reach 50% or more per year for these metals. This level of supply inflation means that they are not good ways to store value. Do not be lured in by rarity when analyzing value. Focus on scarcity.

When a money is not scarce, the supply can be manipulated at will. This is true for both metal and paper money. As an example, assume that the cost of one ton of copper is $5,000. If the price of copper skyrockets because of some unexplained demand, copper miners can easily mine more to meet the increased demand because copper is an abundant metal and is neither rare nor scarce. Since copper miners can flood the market with as much copper as they want, prices eventually fall because supply can meet demand. With gold, this does not happen. If people suddenly want more gold, miners cannot easily mine that much more.

The US dollar is much more like copper than it is like gold. It is neither scarce nor rare. We have the equivalent of one miner, the Federal Reserve, who can flood the market with more dollars whenever they want.

Scarcity has always been the most critical determinant in a money's success, but the success comes with a caveat. If money is too scarce and cannot be easily divided, it will be difficult or impossible to conduct small transactions. This is why, for most of history, silver has actually been the most successful money.

SILVER

SILVER'S HISTORY GOES back almost as far back as gold, with the ancient Egyptians using the metal as well, though it was in Mesopotamia that silver had its first dominant era. As societies became more advanced, silver proved to be a better metal to alternatives like copper due to a higher scarcity, but not as high as gold. Gold was too rare to be used for the most part. Buying a day's worth of food in gold would require such a tiny sliver of metal in payment that it was simply not feasible for most transactions.

Eventually, bimetallism became increasingly popular, with large wealth transferred in gold while small purchases were made in silver. As paper money became increasingly commonplace around the 1600s and was often backed by gold, gold was now more divisible. For the first time, a small item could be purchased using gold in the form of a paper note. Through paper, users were able to gain the benefits of a scarcer money while still enjoying the divisibility for small payments that silver previously provided.

Due to paper money, silver has steadily lost its monetary premium over the last 500 years and is unlikely to get it back. Since humans have figured out ways to make more scarce resources divisible enough to function, silver no longer plays the role that it once did as arguably the most important metal in money's history to date. Today, silver is commonly used as just another industrial metal, though it still has its share of fans and speculators.

US DOLLARS AND SCARCITY

LET US THINK about this scarcity aspect of money some more and compare it to how US dollars work. As was already discussed in previous chapters, the Federal Reserve aims for the US dollar to devalue by 2% per year against the Consumer Price Index (CPI). To get 2% price inflation, though, the Fed almost always needs to print *more* than 2% new dollars every year. An increase in the money supply does not lead to an exact, predictable growth in the CPI. There are always many different economic forces happening at once in an economy.

Like printing new money, some of these forces are inflationary, while others, like an aging population, are deflationary. These forces work against each other and ultimately result in a change in prices.

Regardless of a change in prices though, an increase in new money being printed lowers the value of one dollar itself, since each new unit reduces the value of those already in existence. In recent years, more money has been printed than ever.

Even before 2020, the growth of the money supply had steadily and significantly increased over time, far beyond 2% per year. This growth in the money supply led to the many problems that we have already discussed in these modern money chapters.

There are many different measures for estimating the money supply. M1 includes cash and checking deposits, while M2 contains all elements of M1 as well as "near money." Near money refers to savings deposits, money market securities, mutual funds, and other time deposits. M2 assets are less liquid than M1 and not as suitable as exchange mediums, but they can be quickly converted into cash or checking deposits.

The chart in Figure 1 shows the growth in M2 over time. Take further note of how M2 went vertical in 2020, as the COVID-19 pandemic led to unprecedented levels of stimulus from the Federal Reserve and the US government. The mindset on spending has changed among the public and our leaders, with it being certain that M2 will continue to grow faster than ever in the next decade. And as M2 grows, the value of each individual dollar goes down.

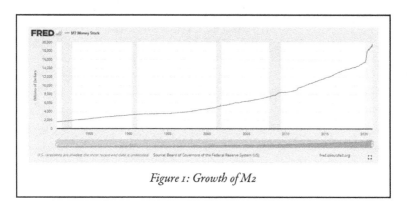

Figure 1: Growth of M2

Contrast the growth of M2 with the supply of gold. The best estimate is that approximately 190,000 tonnes of gold have already been mined and are above ground right now, and the average yearly amount mined in recent years is about 3,000 tonnes.[50]

This is the fundamental value property of gold. You cannot increase the supply at will. Part of what makes gold valuable today is that it has been valued for so long. With gold, the supply is highly limited. There is a lot of gold above the ground already. Humans have been mining it for at least 5,000 years. This is scarcity. You cannot easily increase the supply. Even though mining technology has significantly improved and we are mining more gold than ever, the new increase in the supply of gold is consistently less than 2%, which is a very low inflation rate.

Gold is both a hedge against poor monetary policy while also generally just being a better store of value than the dollar. For example, the chart in Figure 2 shows the rise of college tuition growth over time in gold.

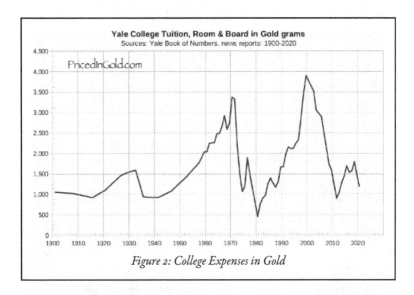

Figure 2: College Expenses in Gold

Everybody has heard that the price of college tuition has been rapidly growing in recent times, but that is only because Americans tend to just think with a dollar-denominated mindset. The chart in Figure 2 shows that when using gold as your base currency, the price of college tuition is not actually near its all-time high. In fact, if you are looking from 1960 on, tuition is cheaper on average than it has been for the last sixty years.

US DOLLARS AND STORE OF VALUE

What exactly does this mean? Simply put, the US dollar is a lousy store of value. It works well as a unit of account and as a medium of exchange, but it fails as a store of value. Dollars lose value every year, by design, as an ever-increasing number of dollars get issued and join the circulating supply. Industries like education do not see the benefits of technological improvements, which make things cheaper, the same way that other industries do. As a result, the higher dollar price of college tuition reflects the dollar's true devaluation over time.

If you want to store your wealth over time in dollars, you cannot do that by keeping your money in the bank since saving is taxed through inflation. You need to find some way to make the money grow. When you have a scarce money, like gold, the form of money in itself *is* the way to maintain your savings. It is not that the price of gold goes up over time, it is that your dollar is *losing* value as many more dollars are created than gold is mined.

People often discourage buying gold by pointing out that investing in the stock market has netted a larger annual return over time than holding gold. This comparison is flawed, however, because gold is not an investment in the traditional sense. Gold is a base layer currency, like the dollar or the euro. Holding gold is not equivalent to investing in a company that is supposed to grow and generate cash flow. By owning gold, an individual chooses to store their savings in a form of money that has better wealth storing properties than a fiat currency. In this way, owning gold is more akin to being an alternative to dollars kept in a savings account than it is to being part of an investment portfolio.

Gold is often misunderstood in modern society. The world has gotten increasingly digital, and so too has its money. The idea that a lump of metal mined from the earth has value for reasons that are still true is so foreign to our way of thinking about money that it becomes difficult to look past. To recognize why gold remains valuable, it is necessary to first understand how modern fiat money works and the many negative trade-offs that have affected society throughout the shift to a fully fiat world.

Modern money is not better than gold in every way. It simply chooses different characteristics of money to prioritize. Instead of scarcity, gold's defining feature, fiat money prioritizes portability and an ability to control the issuance of currency at will. For storing value over time, gold will very likely remain a superior choice to paper money. To the readers who have never given gold much thought prior to this book, perhaps now you have a little more knowledge and respect for the value of the ancient metal of kings.

BEING THE GLOBAL RESERVE CURRENCY

THE UNITED STATES dollar is the global reserve currency. This fact is of tremendous importance. Being the global reserve currency means that the dollar is held by almost all central banks worldwide and is the dominant currency for international settlement. Because of this, many goods that are traded globally are priced in dollars, even when the US is not involved in the trade.

Oil is the most common globally traded good priced in dollars. It is not just in America that the news quotes the price of oil as so many US dollars a barrel. That price is in dollars everywhere. If Germany is buying oil from Saudi Arabia, that transaction will likely be both priced and paid for in dollars. Since every country uses dollars, there is a lot of demand for the US dollar outside of the country.

GIVES THE US POWER

TO START, BEING the global reserve currency means that the US can print more money without it affecting prices in the country as much as it would otherwise. For example, imagine a country where the currency is not highly demanded, such as Nicaragua. Not many countries worldwide transact or hold the Nicaraguan currency, the cordoba. Suppose Nicaragua's central bank printed a significant amount of new money, whether for stimulus or any other reason. The funds would entirely stay within the country since there is minimal global demand for Nicaraguan money. Since the money would remain within the country, but the number of goods and services available would remain static, prices within the country would inevitably rise to reflect the degree of the new money created.

In the United States, this is not the case. Since there is so much outside demand for the dollar from other countries, new money creation does not affect prices in the same way it does for a lesser demanded currency. Because the dollar is the global reserve currency, there is a constant pull of dollars outside of the country. As new money is made, a significant portion of it is pulled outside the system by countries such as China, France, and Russia. Since much of the money leaves the country, there is a reduction in price inflation that occurs from new American money production. Having global reserve status is a decided advantage. New money can be created without having to suffer the same degree of consequences.

Being the global reserve currency allows the US to fund government programs, run chronic budget deficits, and engage in levels of stimulus that are not possible for the rest of the world. With so much global demand for the dollar, we can engage in massive amounts of expansionary money policy while avoiding that policy's worst expected outcomes—something we couldn't avoid if the dollar was demanded at the level of the cordoba. Due to how the economy works, even dollars designed to stay within United States programs end up being pulled out of the country. There is a constant and regular global demand for dollars that reduces the pressures on our monetary system.

Not only does having global reserve currency status provide the US with domestic monetary policy advantages, it also gives the US tremendous power and influence abroad. Since the plurality of international trade is completed in US dollars, it pressures all other countries to stay on the good side of the United States. The US has the power to issue sanctions on countries that effectively cut them off from even participating in global trade. When you control the currency being used, you get to control who gets to use that currency—at least who gets to use that currency in official channels and on traditional payment rails. This allows the US considerable influence globally, and they are not afraid to wield that power.

The dollar formally became the global reserve currency in 1944 after the Bretton Woods Agreement. As discussed earlier, Bretton Woods was a conference in 1944 where delegates from 44 different nations gathered to discuss new rules for a post-World War II monetary system. The outcome of this conference resulted in what was known as the Bretton Woods system, where every country around the world pegged their country's exchange rate to the dollar and the dollar pegged its exchange rate to gold. It was at this point that every country's currency became explicitly linked to the US dollar. Even though the dollar was no longer pegged to gold after 1971, the dollar has still been the world's global reserve currency.

TRUST AND THE AMERICAN ECONOMY

IF THE DOLLAR, or any modern national currency, is no longer a proxy for a valuable metal, how can it function as money if it is just made of worthless paper? Among those who are not educated in monetary history, it is a common refrain to hear that the US dollar maintains its strength through one of a variety of reasons. Whether it is argued that the dollar holds value because of "the strength of the American economy" or "is backed by the military," all arguments in this manner misunderstand what allows money to succeed.

The pivotal trait in money is, of course, scarcity. The dollar is not simply worthless paper. If it were, any individual would be able to create new dollars themselves. As we know, this is not the case. The paper that makes US dollars is not just any paper; it has been designed and imprinted with anti-counterfeit technologies that make it so that only one minter can create new money. The counterfeit-resistant nature allows the paper money to be relatively scarce, far beyond what ordinary paper would allow. In this way, paper money is not just paper. It is potentially scarce because it only has one producer.

This is important to understand—paper money can be just as scarce as gold, provided the currency's new production is limited. The critical differentiator between gold and fiat money, however, is trust. With gold, miners are mining as much gold as they can. It just so happens that the most gold that can be mined in a given year is usually less than 2% of the total supply. With a fiat currency, the miner—the Federal Reserve in the US—is not restricted by what can be physically mined from the earth's crust. While its paper money has the potential to be scarce, the Federal Reserve has to be trusted not to inflate the supply of the currency too high, or else hyperinflation may occur, and the money will collapse.

History has proven that currency minters, either central banks or national governments, cannot remain disciplined enough to keep their currencies scarce. The temptation is too high to print large amounts of new money, accidentally devaluing the money in the process. In this way, fiat currencies' history is similar to that of ancient coins made of inferior, abundant monetary metals such as copper or bronze. Over time, the constant high flow of new money creation ends up breaking the system. This is why gold has managed to maintain value even in a fiat currency world, although gold and silver have certainly had their issues with coin clipping and devaluation as well. Whereas fiat currencies require trust, gold is limited by miner production.

All currency is valuable because of its ability to meet the five properties of money—divisibility, durability, portability, recognizability, and scarcity. The switch from gold to fiat currency was first a switch from prioritizing absolute scarcity in the currency to portability, which secondly allowed for maximum control over the money itself. As has been seen throughout history, that control over money has rarely resulted in good outcomes.

All countries follow a similar fiat system globally, so why is the American dollar the most highly regarded? The reason is trust. Fiat currencies require trust. Almost all currencies have failed throughout history, and typically for one of three reasons. The first reason is through war. When a state falls, the currency often falls with it. The second reason currencies fail is through a gradual shift from abundant money to more scarce money, such as the natural shift to the silver shekel becoming the dominant monetary unit in Mesopotamia. The third reason that currencies fail—and the one that most directly has to do with human management—is hyperinflation. When given the ability to increase the money supply at will, with the only restraint being discipline, this discipline will eventually erode, and the currency supply will hyperinflate.

First and foremost, this is why the US dollar is the global reserve currency today. Globally, there is the most faith that the US government and Federal Reserve are the least likely of any country to destroy the money through mismanagement.

This faith is compounded further by the power of the US economy. As mentioned earlier, there is more global demand for dollars than there is for any other international currency. The United States is a mass producer and consumer, although the country imports significantly more than it exports. The fact that the nation demands so many goods from across the world is a key component of the global economy. Measured by GDP, the US is the largest economy in the world. This allows the United States to have more leeway with its monetary policy than other countries. Dollars are driven out of the country, which alleviates the inflationary pressure that is the direct cause of so many currency collapses.

While the US has this extra leniency, it also has a relatively conservative history with monetary policy. The Federal Reserve, the United States' central bank, is an independent entity, meaning it is not a government body. While the President does nominate new chairs of the Federal Reserve, the institution is supposed to be isolated from the rest of the government, allowing it to focus on one goal—keeping the dollar functioning correctly. While this independence deserves to be scrutinized, and indeed the Fed has acted as a political body in many cases, there is no doubt that the United States' Federal Reserve has done a better job managing the currency than many other central banks worldwide. When it comes to managing a currency, being conservative is typically superior to being overly loose or political.

The combination of the trust in the Federal Reserve and the strength of the US economy drives the value of the dollar. The many benefits granted from having global reserve currency status allow the US to create new money at a rate that other countries cannot. The balance only works as long as the rest of the world both trusts the controllers of the printing press and has continued belief in the American economy.

TESTING TRUST

WHAT IS HAPPENING now is that the Federal Reserve is beginning to push the limits of that trust. Over the course of the decade between 2009-2019, interest rates steadily fell. It reached a point where rates were near zero, even though the economy had become relatively strong. In late 2018, the Federal Reserve attempted to raise interest rates, which was met with strong rejection from financial markets. The message was clear. The economy could not survive with higher interest rates, and rates were subsequently lowered again.

Along with the decade-long lowering of interest rates was the Fed's quantitative easing program in the wake of the 2008 recession. Instead of being restricted in monetary easing through manipulating interest rates, the Fed created additional new money by purchasing longer-term securities from sources on the open market, which further added to the money supply and encouraged market participants to borrow. Before 2020, monetary policy in the US had become expansionary in a way that had never quite been seen before. Then the COVID-19 pandemic happened.

With the onset of the Coronavirus pandemic in early 2020, the economy faced its first major shock in over a decade. Millions of jobs were lost, and the economy came to a standstill as stringent lockdowns were imposed on businesses and individuals alike. To minimize the permanent damage to the economy, the Federal Reserve jumped into action by unleashing the printing presses further, getting as much new money flowing into the economy as possible to spark productive economic activity.

With interest rates already at zero, however, the Federal Reserve was limited in its actions, even with quantitative easing. When monetary policy is at its limits, the federal government often steps into the picture, which is precisely what happened in 2020. Seeing the catastrophic effects of COVID-19 and the subsequent lockdowns, a massive economic stimulus bill was passed. This resulted in more new money entering the economy than has happened at any point in the country's history. In fact, more money was created in June 2020 alone than in the first 200 years of the United States' existence.[51]

There are several interesting factors at play here. The United States dwarfs the rest of the world when it comes to sheer monetary stimulus. Nobody is creating new money quite like the US. This tests the trust that allows our currency to keep its global reserve status. Indeed, other countries are increasingly growing skeptical of relying on the dollar. In 2019, the dollar was at its lowest share of global currency reserves since 2013.[52] There is a growing fear that the dollar may no longer be as reliable as it once was as constant monetary stimulus seems to have no end in sight.

If the dollar lost its global reserve status, the outcomes would be significant. Having global reserve status is the largest reason the US is able to run the government deficits that it can without inflation rising. Much of the new money that is created ends up leaving the country since the dollar is so highly demanded across the globe, which alleviates the inflationary pressure that naturally arises from new money creation.

Losing reserve currency status would make it impossible

for the levels of spending that occur now to continue. If spending did not decrease significantly, price levels would rise sharply, because all of the deficit-financed spending would stay within the country's borders. Budgets would need to be heavily slashed to avoid this.

Losing reserve status would be a problem that could not be solved by a simple solution such as increasing taxes on the wealthy. The reality is, however, that it is unlikely spending would be cut sufficiently. Budgets are highly political, and there would not be adequate support to cut enough funding. It is much more likely that deficit spending will continue, with Main Street Americans paying the price through inflation.

Part of the reason it may be difficult for some to comprehend losing this status is because being the global reserve currency is outside the control that Americans can exert. It is not up to voters. Most Americans do not even realize the privileges they have been awarded due to living under the global reserve currency. Instead, the global reserve status is based on trust between nations, and that trust is being eroded.

For those who rely on the dollar remaining the global reserve currency, there is still reason to stay hopeful. While there are many issues with the dollar, there is no clear alternative or challenger to the dollar's throne. After the dollar, the top two choices for fiat monetary supremacy would likely be the euro and the Chinese renminbi. Regardless of all the troubles with the dollar, these two currencies do not fare much better.

CHALLENGERS TO THE DOLLAR

WHILE THE EURO may not operate with deficits quite on

the United States' scale, the European Central Bank (ECB) has enacted a monetary agenda that is even more extreme in some respects, namely with regards to negative interest rates.

Negative interest rates are exactly what they sound like. If you store your money in the bank, not only do you not receive interest payments on your deposits, but the depositor actually has to pay the bank to keep their money. While this may sound ludicrous to the average American, the idea is simply a continuation of the trend of interest rate reduction policy.

When interest rates are dropped, people and businesses are more inclined to take out loans from the bank since the cost of money is lower. When interest rates go below zero, it means that the person taking out the loan has to pay back less than the principal. For example, if you take a $100,000 loan in a negative interest rate world using a rate of -1%, you would only need to repay $99,000. Even before the introduction of negative interest rates, modern money already penalized savers to encourage more debt. By bringing interest rates into the negative, savers are penalized in a way that has not previously been seen in modern banking.

The reason that rates have gone so far as to be negative is the constantly increasing economic dependence on debt. The economy cannot sustain itself without increasing debt, as has been previously discussed. This is as true for Europe as it is for the United States. It is even more of a problem for the Europeans as the European Union generally has a weaker overall economy than that of the United States, which has led the ECB to take extreme measures to prevent the debt bubble from bursting. As with the United States, however, the problem has gotten so severe that the only solution to stop the bubble is to encourage even more debt to prevent a depression. By constantly increasing debt, we kick the can down the road and make the problem worse for the future.

The Federal Reserve of the United States has claimed that interest rates will not go negative. While this is a noble thing to say, there is reason to be cynical. Interest rates in the US are already essentially zero, which means that there is limited additional ammo for the Fed to encourage borrowing further. While the Fed can and will continue to engage in quantitative easing, the adjustment of interest rates has long been its predominant tool for affecting monetary policy. With rates already at zero and it being improbable that they will be raised any time soon—due to the extreme levels of debt that would be defaulted on if this occurred—the Fed is faced with limited options. While they insist otherwise, it seems inevitable that negative interest rates are coming eventually. Regardless, they are not here yet the way they are with the EU.

The euro faces trouble for more reasons as well. The entire European Union is teetering, as it becomes increasingly difficult to manage its member nations' needs and desires. There is a clear divide between those countries in a relatively healthy financial and economic position and those heavily indebted and with poorer economies. In the EU, it is up to the economically strong countries to hold up the weak, which is the source of much tension. Countries that need a combination of fiscal stimulus and a looser monetary policy are at odds with those whose healthy economies that might require a tighter monetary policy.

One monetary policy to manage twenty-seven countries is difficult to oversee, and unrest with the situation has been growing. Interestingly, the countries that are most fed up with the EU are the nations with weaker economic states. Nations with high debt and stalled economies, such as

Greece and Italy, feel that they are not being helped enough by the countries in better financial situations. There is increasing dissatisfaction among EU member states' civilians, and there is the possibility that the EU may break apart. Following the UK's lead, it would not be a surprise to see more nations vote to leave the European Union.

This all posits that the euro is not likely a superior choice than the dollar for achieving global reserve status. There is too much uncertainty that comes with the need to collaboratively manage the economies of twenty-seven member nations. Certain countries will always benefit at others' expense. Furthermore, the region has already implemented a highly aggressive quantitative easing and negative interest rate policy, the latter of which goes beyond what the United States has attempted. While indeed one of the world's strongest currencies, the euro still has shakier fundamentals than that of the dollar.

There is only one other dominant nation that would pose a threat to US dollar hegemony—China. China has a rapidly growing economy, about four times the United States' population, and is increasingly doing everything it can to solidify itself as the greatest world power. There is good reason to believe that the Chinese economy will eventually surpass the US in GDP as a nation. While the US still produces about 33% more than China, China's much larger population gives the country a significant advantage in national, nominal GDP numbers.[53] Since there are so many more Chinese people than Americans, it would only take a GDP per capita of one-third of China's American value to overtake the US in national GDP. Observing the two nations' trends over the last decade makes it clear that this is indeed possible.

While China's economy may continue to grow faster

than the United States', it is difficult to imagine that much of the world would embrace Chinese currency for global settlement. The Chinese government can be quite hostile to US and European interests, partially due to resentment of the developed West's global dominance over the previous few centuries. China simply has its own way of doing things, which does not always coincide with Western desires.

Furthermore, China is not a free country. Almost all payments and text messages are made through the mobile application WeChat, owned by the massive multinational conglomerate Tencent Holdings Limited. This app is essentially spyware that monitors all the payments and text messages between Chinese citizens. If the government sees something that they do not like, they take action.

This action comes in many forms, of which a few can be highlighted from the Free Hong Kong protests in 2019. During this time, many protesters were using WeChat to organize or simply discuss the ongoing protests. Users of the app found that their messages were being censored and deleted, and text groups that had formed were expunged with no explanation.[54] Many protesters realized the danger of speaking too freely using WeChat but overlooked the application's financial surveillance aspect. When attending protests, many used the payment function of WeChat to pay for subway fare that would take them towards protest locations. These people were later tracked through their payments and arrested.

Combining these factors, it seems unlikely that the Western world would adopt Chinese money to be the global reserve currency, but there is only so much that the US and Europe can do. China will undoubtedly remain a powerful force, and its economy is growing larger by the day.

One possibility is that no one currency will dominate

globally. The US and Europe would continue to use the dollar and the euro, while the West's enemies, like Russia and much of the Middle East, might gravitate towards China and the renminbi. Even in this scenario, global dollar demand would decrease, putting higher inflationary pressure on US prices domestically. Still, it is not probable that China will obtain sole global reserve status.

If neither the euro nor the renminbi threatens the dollar's status as the global reserve currency, then what would? There are two likely possibilities.

GENUINELY GLOBAL MONEY

THE FIRST OPTION is that a new currency could be created, a truly global currency. The economist John Maynard Keynes first proposed this idea in the early 1940s, with the currency tentatively named the "bancor." The tender did not come to fruition, and, instead, the world decided to use the dollar as the global reserve currency with the adoption of the Bretton Woods system. In 2009, at a UN G20 summit, the Russians proposed the idea of a new world currency again, operating at a super-sovereign level, managed by the United Nations as a whole. The proposal did not make it far and was not seriously considered, but that it was introduced at all highlighted that some dissatisfaction with the dollar as the world reserve currency is not new.

Since 2009, trust in the dollar has fallen even further, mainly because of the constant, and seemingly endless, monetary stimulus the US government and the Federal Reserve exercise. The United States would never willingly agree to create a new global currency, as it would erode much of their global power. However, if enough of the world decided to make it happen, it remains possible that a new bancor-like currency could be introduced.

If the first option represents all of the world's governments coming together to introduce a world currency above the national level, the second alternative means the opposite—a money of all the world's individuals. Introduced in 2009, Bitcoin is a decentralized, peer-to-peer, digital cash. Much like the Internet itself, Bitcoin is not controlled by any company. There is no person, no issuing body, and no government that controls the currency. It is decentralized. The monetary policy is fixed, meaning it cannot be changed. We will discuss Bitcoin in more detail in the following chapters.

The issue that all national currencies face is that of control. As shown throughout monetary history, when money is manipulated or devalued through improper management, societies collapse and fail. Even today, when most countries are not outright failing, there is often a battle to control currency issuance. Right now, the dollar has the most power, but it may not be that way forever.

In a world where the bancor is controlled by the United Nations, there would likely be regular fighting and political maneuvering to gain more control over the policy guiding the currency. The ability to manage a currency is both a positive and negative. There is the potential to use monetary policy well, to aid struggling countries, and help the global economy. There is also significant risk. If monetary policy is abused, or the currency falls to political infighting, the entire global economy will suffer. History has shown that the latter is likely to occur eventually.

A decentralized currency removes that control. While the monetary policy rules would not be able to be changed to provide aid, the downside risk is also eliminated. A decentralized currency with a fixed monetary policy can be resistant to corruption and be truly neutral in a way that a national currency or a global bancor could never be.

To summarize this chapter, Americans' relationship with the dollar is not as straightforward as most believe. Instead of the dollar being a simple tool that can be relied upon for all trade, the dollar's value is delicately balanced across a multitude of geopolitical factors, including the entire global economy. Too often, Americans discuss problems as simply being a matter of Republican or Democrat, but this thinking is both shallow and too American-centric. The dollar's role is complex, and while it may be America's national currency, it is influenced by factors that are outside of America's control.

It is a shame that a basic understanding of money is not taught in American schools, even in economics classes at the university level. The importance of a society's currency itself has been a deciding factor in almost every civilization's success and failure throughout history, excluding those that were directly conquered. Yet, economists and politicians ignore the role that the dollar itself plays in the economic systems using it.

This understanding is important, because the position of the dollar in the global economy is beginning to shift. The world outside America is becoming increasingly ready to move beyond the dollar. America will do everything it can to prevent that from happening, likely with Europe as its ally, but the outcome seems inevitable. The dissatisfaction with the power that the United States can wield through the dollar has been growing for decades, and the COVID-19 pandemic may represent a breaking point.

While many countries have not been happy with the United States' power, the trust in its economy and monetary policy remained. This is increasingly no longer the case, and faith in the dollar's conservative management is likely permanently eroded—and deservedly so. The main advantage that the dollar continues to have is that no other country can boast a superior monetary policy at this point. Indeed, most critiques of the dollar come from those who have inferior national currencies themselves. Regardless, it is likely that an alternative currency with superior properties will eventually emerge, if it has not already.

As the dollar loses global importance, the American economy will need to change as well, as it will not receive the privileges that it has had for many years. Given the increasing levels of partisanship in government and the overall lack of knowledge about monetary history, it is unlikely that the government will be able to adapt accordingly. As deficits and debts continue to grow, but global demand for the dollar drops, the US economy will suffer. Inflation and wealth inequality will rise further, resulting in even further blame at the partisan level, even though the problem's roots run much deeper.

It may not happen for ten years, or maybe fifty, but the decline of the US dollar as the global reserve currency must be monitored.

PART III:
THE FUTURE OF
MONEY

BITCOIN

WHILE MOST OF us are comfortable with how modern banking works, the truth is that dealing with digital payments and banks today is cumbersome, slow, and difficult. The banking system of 2020 is not much different than it was in 1970. Technology has improved a hundred times since then, yet the way that our money works remains the same. Only within the last decade has this begun to change, and the possibilities for how money may evolve in the future are becoming more apparent. The catalyst for this change, the spark that started the fire and thrust monetary development into the future? Bitcoin.

MONEY AS A TECHNOLOGY

TO TRULY COMPREHEND how Bitcoin represents an evolution in money as a technology, it is necessary to first understand how money itself works, the role that money plays in society, and the issues that have popped up in modern society as a direct result of how modern money works. *The Story of Money* has discussed many of these problems in detail. The final piece of this picture is to discuss money as a technology. Money has always been technology, even when money was just shells, stones, or metal. Money is a human invention, a technology that allows people to store value throughout time.

In the evolution of money as technology, modern society

has shifted from physical coins and paper notes to digital payments managed by banking institutions and financial technology companies. This breaks an essential link between people and the money that they use.

Coins and paper fiat money are bearer instruments, meaning that they themselves have value. When you have coins or dollar bills in your home, you own the money yourself and are the sole owner of the money. While it may sound trivial, this must be mentioned because of how digital payments have developed. Digital money today, money that you store in the bank, is *not* a bearer asset. You are not in possession of, nor do you truly own savings that is kept in a bank. Instead, you hold a promise, an IOU, that the bank will give you your money if you ask for it.

The key here is that modern banking requires trust. A depositor needs to trust that their bank will store their money safely and allow them to transact whenever the depositor sees fit. Cash requires no trust, as whoever is holding the dollar bill has the wealth itself. This model extends even further when considering that the number of intermediaries needed to engage in digital payments goes beyond just the banking institutions themselves. To transfer currency digitally today is to engage in a process involving many different agents, all of whom collect users' data. To put it simply, holding modern digital money is nothing like holding cash itself.

If I want to pay you, or anyone, without using physical cash, there is currently no way to do that without going through a financial go-between. A depositor's savings are held at one intermediary, a bank, and processing payments involves multiple additional liaisons on both sides of the transaction. Using credit and debit cards requires going through both the bank and the payment processor, such as MasterCard or Visa. As financial applications such as Venmo, Zelle, or Cash App have become increasingly popular methods for sending payments, an additional intermediary is added to the mix. Every time a digital payment is made, a bank, Mastercard or Visa, and Venmo all get every piece of information about your transaction, which is then used to build a complete profile about the user.

On October 31, 2008, a person or group of people using the name Satoshi Nakamoto sent a white paper on a cryptography mailing list detailing a new digital cash idea called "Bitcoin." The concept behind Bitcoin was digital cash—to make digital payments more like handing someone dollar bills directly than swiping a credit card that needs to be processed by multiple intermediaries.

What is important to realize is that the ability to send a payment through the Internet, without routing it through any intermediary or company, has never existed before. This is how Bitcoin revolutionized the concept of digital money.

Bitcoin was not the first attempt at digital money. There were many before it. Bitcoin is the culmination of decades of research, advancements in cryptography, and finding solutions to problems that caused other projects to fail in the past.

In 1989, computer scientist and cryptographer David Chaum founded an electronic money corporation called *Digicash Inc.* Digicash was created to make digital payments private so that no bank or government could trace transactions. The company remained active for a decade but eventually filed for bankruptcy in 1999. The problem for Digicash was adoption. It was not easy to get users for the platform or shop owners to accept the Digicash.

The failure of Digicash highlights an obvious issue when trying to create a new form of money—how could a business *create* a money? How could anyone trust it? While your first thought might be to question how privately issued money could be valuable, that is not the issue at hand. Remember, money has specific properties: divisibility, durability, portability, recognizability, and scarcity. Anything that meets these five traits has the potential to be a good form of money, though the best form tends to win out and dominate in the long run.

Still, modern money, like the dollar, fits these traits reasonably well. Unless a new competitor can offer a significant improvement in some fashion, it will be challenging to convince users to adopt a new money. This is particularly true if there is no incentive for the user to adopt the money.

Another attempt at digital money was *e-gold*, created by Gold and Silver Reserve Inc. in 1996. If a user started an account on the company's website, they could purchase a digital currency denominated in grams of gold and be able to make instant transfers to other users of the platform. This was another centralized platform under the control of one company, but unlike Digicash, e-gold gained a notable following.

At its peak in 2006, there was more than $2 billion worth of transactions in e-gold being conducted throughout the year.[55] The primary users of the e-gold platform were online merchants, online casinos, political organizations, and non-profit groups. E-gold was effective in this sense. While units were dominated in grams of gold, it was possible to send payments as small as one ten-thousandth of a gram, effectively being the world's first micro-payment platform. The company even published its payment statistics publicly and revealed that hundreds of thousands of micro-transactions were made daily. This was particularly valuable to international users of e-gold and allowed the platform to grow its global base substantially.

Unfortunately for its users, e-gold's popularity was also the cause of its demise. After the Patriot Act was passed in the US following the 9/11 terrorist attack, it became a crime to operate a money transmitter business without a license. While the company tried for many years to work with regulations to understand how to keep its system afloat, its efforts failed. Due to the platform's nature, Gold and Silver Reserve Inc. faced accusations that e-gold was being used to conduct criminal activity. In 2005, the Justice Department indicted the Gold and Silver Reserve Inc. directors on four counts of violating money laundering regulations and knowingly allowing a transaction involving the purchase of child pornography. E-gold was forced to shut down.

The failure of Digicash and the eventual shutdown of e-gold reveal the crucial point of failure with modern, non-governmental currencies—centralization. Simply being issued by a private company limits any faith that the users of a new form of money would have since if the company failed or was shut down, the currency would fail alongside it. As long as a non-sovereign form of money was centralized, it would not be able to work.

National governments can issue currency as a centralized party because they hold a relative monopoly in their jurisdictions. This works in nations where faith in the government is relatively high. Even now in the United States, where trust in government institutions may be lower than ever, there is still no doubt among most citizens that the safest place for currency to be issued is with the government. This luxury is not true for much of the world, where billions of people do not have a stable money to rely on.

DECENTRALIZATION

BITCOIN HAS SUCCEEDED where other non-sovereign currencies have failed due to this realization that decentralization is the key to make it work. When a person transacts using Bitcoin, there is no intermediary at all. There is no person, group of people, or company that is "in charge" of Bitcoin. In this way, Bitcoin is like the Internet, a decentralized protocol. What Satoshi Nakamoto did in 2009 was create computer code that anybody on the Internet could download. As long as one person downloaded the open-source code to run the Bitcoin network, Bitcoin could operate. Over time, Bitcoin has become gradually more and more decentralized. There are now tens of thousands of people running Bitcoin, located worldwide, that keep the network running and distributed.

The way that Satoshi was able to create this system was through the creation of what is now called a "blockchain." A blockchain is essentially a database that keeps a record of all the transactions that have ever happened on Bitcoin. There are a few components that make up the Bitcoin blockchain and work together to keep the network operational and decentralized. The two main components of the Bitcoin blockchain are called miners and nodes.

Think of a blockchain as an empty notebook that will eventually be filled with every user's transactions. Each empty page of the book represents a block of the blockchain. Miners are the people who write the transactions down on each page, filling up the pages of the blockchain book. In Bitcoin, a block is processed every ten minutes on average. For our example, this means that a new page of the notebook is written every ten minutes.

Then there are nodes. Nodes make sure that what the

miners are writing down on the pages tracks with what has happened in past pages. Nodes track the entire history of the blockchain. This process all works together to create the Bitcoin network.

Bitcoin is a protocol, meaning a set of rules and standards. The Internet is also a protocol. Have you ever tried to explain either to yourself or others what the Internet is? Likely, you do not know how to describe it. The Internet is a set of standards for how computers can communicate with one another. When you connect to the Internet, your computer connects to other computers using the TCP/IP protocol. The protocol itself is a base layer, a means of communication, which allowed for the Internet that we see every day to be built on top of. The protocol layer is the base, and then you build on top of it. Bitcoin is a protocol for digital money. In this way, it is not just that Bitcoin is "Internet money." It is much more. Bitcoin is the Internet *of* money.

Part of what Satoshi was able to do that makes Bitcoin unique was create an inventive structure that encourages others to adopt Bitcoin as a currency. There are tens of thousands of people mining Bitcoin around the world. Mining Bitcoin is computer-intensive and requires cheap power to perform profitably. While it used to be possible to mine on a standard household computer, it now requires specialized equipment. Since mining requires a good deal of work, Satoshi put in place an incentive structure that encouraged early adopters to participate in mining.

Bitcoin has a fixed monetary policy. There will only ever be 21 million Bitcoin. Starting at zero, every ten minutes on average, new Bitcoin is created at a fixed rate. Every four years, the amount of Bitcoin that is created is cut in half. This happens until 2140, at which point no new Bitcoin will ever be created. There is no Federal Reserve, no bank, no individual, or group of people that can ever change this.

To incentivize miners, they compete with one another to mine each Bitcoin block through a process known as "proof-of-work." Whichever miner succeeds at mining the Bitcoin block is rewarded with the new issuance of Bitcoin. At the time of writing, with one BTC (Bitcoin's ticker symbol) at $35,000 and the block reward at 6.25—meaning that 6.25 new Bitcoin are issued with each block—miners collectively earn $218,750 every ten minutes (on average). By incorporating this structure, Satoshi gave miners the incentive to bootstrap the network in its early stages.

Complementing miners are nodes. While miners mine Bitcoin blocks, pushing the blockchain forward, nodes verify all the transactions included in each block to make sure that they follow the Bitcoin protocol rules. Nodes make sure that people cannot spend money that they do not have. This system has worked very well. Throughout Bitcoin's lifespan, there has never been a counterfeit Bitcoin.

Unlike with miners, there is no economic incentive to run a node, but it is also much easier to run a node than a miner. No specialized equipment is needed, and a node can run in the background on any modern computer. Nodes neither consume significant energy nor slow down your computer at all, with just a simple computer application needing to be downloaded to get started. This makes it very easy to run a node.

The importance of nodes on the Bitcoin network's decentralization cannot be overstated, though most of the attention finds itself being on the flashier miners. Because of the role of nodes, there has never been a counterfeit Bitcoin.

This also highlights a significant improvement that Bitcoin has over gold—the cost of verification. If a vendor receives a gold coin for whatever reason, there are few ways to verify that it is actual gold. There have been countless attempts to counterfeit gold throughout its entire history. Even today, gold-plated bars filled with tungsten are regularly found.[56] The reason for this is that gold is very costly to verify.

Have you ever seen movies where a person bites a gold coin to confirm that it is authentic, since gold is relatively malleable? This may work to a degree with small coins, but it does not work with larger bars, and it certainly does not work at scale. Testing the purity of gold cannot quickly be done at home without somewhat expensive equipment and, even then, with only a certain amount of reliability.

A Bitcoin node, then, is like being able to verify gold for nearly no cost at all. Anyone with an Internet connection, a computer (and soon, a cell phone), and downloaded software can run a node. The software is not computer-intensive and allows the user to verify their own transactions. Crucially, no one person *needs* to run a Bitcoin node. You are not required to participate in the consensus process and do not need to run a node if you are not interested in doing so. There are tens of thousands of Bitcoin nodes spread worldwide, all verifying that all transactions on the network are valid and not counterfeit.

Because of this extreme level of decentralization, no individual is required to run any special software to run or verify the Bitcoin network. Instead, since there are no central points of failure, the trust-minimized way that Bitcoin operates ensures that any user can transact with any other user in complete confidence that there will be no fraudulent transactions. Still, what makes Bitcoin unique is that any person *can* verify this for themselves, and many do. The ease with which it is possible to run a Bitcoin node highlights one of its great strengths when compared to gold. Where gold is very costly to verify, Bitcoin is incredibly cheap. This ease in verification promotes Bitcoin's most important trait—decentralization.

The importance of decentralization cannot be overemphasized when talking about Bitcoin. It is in the background of everything that has to do with the protocol. As has been seen throughout history, if a system has the potential to be corrupted, eventually it will be. Most forms of money have failed due to a lack of scarcity, which can either result from natural causes or human manipulation. Bitcoin was designed with these past failures in mind and was launched to prevent them from reoccurring. Apart from decentralization, the two principles that make Bitcoin different from what has come before are sound money and censorship resistance.

SOUND MONEY

BITCOIN HAS A fixed monetary policy. There will only ever be 21 million Bitcoin. In 2009 when the network launched, there were zero Bitcoin circulating, with new Bitcoin being created through mining. Every ten minutes on average, new Bitcoin enters circulation at a fixed rate. The amount of Bitcoin created divided by two every four years. In 2140, all this activity will stop and no new Bitcoin will be mined. Nothing can ever change this—no federal reserve, no bank, no individual, nor group of people. This is interesting in a few different ways. Nothing like this has ever existed before. Secured by what is known as cryptography and its decentralized properties, Bitcoin has a level of unforgeable scarcity that has never been seen in any money before.

"Digital scarcity" is a concept that had not existed before

Bitcoin. The idea can be difficult for people to grasp. For nearly all of our digital history, files could simply be copied. If one person wanted to send a PDF file to another friend or colleague, they would attach the file to an e-mail and send it off. Now there are two copies of the file. Certain companies might go to extreme measures, such as using Digital Rights Management (DRM), to prevent unauthorized redistribution of digital media, but the files themselves could still be copied. This is how our mind works when we think about digital things, and our first instinct may be to be suspicious when attempting to understand how something digital could also be valuable.

The ability to make Bitcoin counterfeit-resistant in a decentralized way is part of why what Satoshi did with Bitcoin is so unique. Through the proof-of-work mining process, with transactions validated by nodes, Satoshi created the first cryptographically secured and provably scarce digital asset in existence. Other than Bitcoin, there are *still* no other truly scarce digital assets, except other crypto networks that followed Satoshi's lead.

With a 21 million supply cap, Bitcoin is the scarcest asset on earth that is also sufficiently divisible, durable, portable, and recognizable. Detractors will often mention that just because something is scarce does not mean that it is valuable, but this is a misunderstanding of the properties of money. Ask a person to name an item that is scarce but *also* easily divisible and transferable, and they will struggle to think of one. If you could take the Mona Lisa, break it into tiny pieces—without reducing its value by doing so—and digitally transfer it across the planet without any intermediaries. There would only be one Mona Lisa, and each user would own a small fraction of it. That is like Bitcoin. Scarcity may not be inherently valuable, but scarcity that can be divided and transferred absolutely is. That is Bitcoin.

Being scarce on its own is not enough, however. Recall that silver was the dominant metal used throughout most of money's history, not gold. While gold has always been scarcer, it was actually too scarce to function well as money in nearly all early civilizations. Since it was so rare, gold could not work as a medium of exchange for small transactions. It would be impossible to chip off a piece of gold or create a gold coin that would be small enough for purchases of everyday items like corn or rice. Silver fit this role better for much of history. Through its protocol, Bitcoin has a scarcity beyond gold while simultaneously being more divisible than either silver or the dollar today.

Furthermore, it is essential to understand the difference between centralized rarity and protocol-level scarcity. Many goods can be rare. If Louis Vuitton launched a limited-edition handbag where only 1,000 would be created and sold, there would surely be a rush among the wealthy to be one of the few who could lay a claim to such a rare purse. Since Louis Vuitton is a highly demanded brand, there would certainly be 1,000 people willing to pay a high price for one of these rare, limited-edition bags. This is entirely artificial scarcity, however. If Louis Vuitton desired to make more of the same purse in the future, nothing is stopping them from doing so. The supply can be inflated at any time. It is just a matter of whether the decision-makers at Louis Vuitton choose to do so or not.

Throughout this book we've followed the definitions of rarity and scarcity where rarity represents the total or absolute amount of a good available, while scarcity is the degree to which it is possible to increase the supply of the good. One thousand Louis Vuitton purses may be rare, but they are not scarce. Scarcity, not rarity, is the critical characteristic for a form of money to maintain its value throughout time because scarcity is what determines the potential dilution of the money supply. If only ten Louis Vuitton purses were made each year instead of 1,000, but the supply doubled each year, the bags would still be rare, but still not scarce, since the inflation rate on purses would be 100%.

Bitcoin, on the other hand, has scarcity written into its protocol layer. The supply will never go beyond the 21 million cap that is in its computer code. Since the scarcity is defined within the Bitcoin protocol itself, there is no trust required, as in the example with Louis Vuitton.

This is interesting in a few different ways. Nothing like it has ever existed before. Secured by cryptography, which is akin to computer mathematics, as well as through its decentralized properties, Bitcoin has a level of unforgeable scarcity that has never been seen in any type of money before. Think about gold's properties as a store of value and how its scarcity has allowed it to stay valuable for thousands of years. Bitcoin has none of the history of gold but was explicitly created with those properties in mind. If you can understand the value proposition of owning gold, you are already about 75% of the way there with Bitcoin.

Bitcoin is also essentially infinitely divisible, with the smallest unit, known as a satoshi—a sat for short—being one one-hundred-millionth of a Bitcoin. This divisibility is important because it fixes one of the biggest problems gold has as money. Today, a $200 gold coin might be the size of a dime. There is simply no way to buy a pack of gum for gold, as the gold piece would just be too small. With Bitcoin, the smallest unit can buy goods that cost a penny or even less. Bitcoin's divisibility opens up the possibility for a micropayment economy to develop, which will be briefly discussed later in this chapter.

There are often discussions about gold and Bitcoin that debate whether the two assets can meaningfully coexist. Since gold's primary value stems from its scarcity, the comparison is valid. However, even though gold is scarce compared to most other assets, Bitcoin's 21 million cap represents the first absolutely scarce money in history.

Gold bugs often mention that gold is physically tangible and has use in various industries. These are not strengths for gold; they are weaknesses. The physicality of gold results in its greatest failing as money as it is not easily transferable. Transferring physical gold is costly and requires trust in a custodian to transfer the gold (in most cases). On the other hand, Bitcoin can be sent globally, near-instantly, and with no third-party intermediary. Bitcoin's lack of physicality is a feature, not a bug, which is why the potential for confiscation is much higher with gold than Bitcoin.

Due to the difficulty in transporting, storing, and verifying gold, the supply of the metal has become highly centralized. Most the world's gold is currently in central banks and government vaults, with a much smaller tonnage circulating on the market and stored by private individuals. Throughout history, precious metal banks, vaults, and custodians are among the first places captured once a military conquest or war has been won. With Bitcoin, as long as you keep your private seed phrase safe—which can even be memorized—your Bitcoin cannot be confiscated.

Over the long run, there should be room for gold and Bitcoin to coexist. Given that the combined size of bonds, equities, and real estate is more than $150 trillion, and many institutional funds are underweight in gold, gold as a reasonably scarce physical asset is still likely undervalued in global markets.

Sound money means a money that is reliable in function and resistant to manipulation. With a sound form of money, a user can rely on the fact that the rules of the currency will not change. Through math, aka cryptography, we now have an asset that cannot ever be inflated, which you can also send across the globe almost instantly, without going through any intermediary. The rules were set at the start of Bitcoin's launch, and they will remain the same as long as Bitcoin's blockchain keeps producing blocks. Bitcoin's static monetary policy, built around the idea of sound money, is something that has never been seen before in monetary history.

CENSORSHIP RESISTANCE

CENSORSHIP RESISTANCE IS the characteristic that everyone using the Bitcoin network is equal. Anybody, at any time, can send a transaction to anyone they choose, and the transaction will go through. The system is tamper-proof. No third party, like a company or a government, can restrict or prevent you from transacting with someone.

According to the Human Rights Foundation, more than 50% of the world's population lives under an authoritarian regime. For these people, often living under ruthless dictators and human rights abusers, Bitcoin can be a valuable financial tool as a censorship-resistant medium of exchange.

Think of China, a country whose government monitors nearly everything its citizens do. During the Free Hong Kong protests, many protesters had to take the subway to attend the demonstrations. Since metropolitan Hong Kong has significantly reduced the amount of cash that is used as money, most protesters used their WeChat Pay apps to pay for subway fare. As the Chinese government cracked down on the protests, people who used their WeChat apps to pay for subway fare were later tracked down and arrested.

Even in the US, workers in legal industries like pawn shops, pornography sales, marijuana stores, and online gambling businesses are often denied the right to use banks at all, which is incredibly dangerous. This denial of essential financial services can be credited to what is known as "Operation Choke Point" in 2013. Operation Choke Point was a coordinated effort by the Department of Justice (DoJ) to exclude millions of Americans from the banking system. The DoJ began thoroughly investigating banks that held accounts for any people who worked in one of the aforementioned industries, claiming that these industries often engaged in financial crimes like fraud and money laundering.

These actions directly led to the exclusion of workers in these industries from the banking system, and the undemocratic process in which this exclusion took place should be noted. Instead of dealing with the hassle of the investigations, banks simply closed the accounts, essentially making banking with these workers illegal without actually passing any laws. While less extreme than in many other countries worldwide, the US is not immune to using financial censorship as a means of control and oppression. Since Operation Choke Point began, the homicide rate of sex workers has increased by over 400%.[57]

Throughout 2020, the country of Belarus was engaged in political turmoil over a contested election result. Belarus President, Alexander Lukashenko, essentially a dictator, supposedly won the election with 80% of the vote. Much of the larger world did not accept the election results, with it appearing quite likely the election was not free and fair.

Thousands of protesters gathered in Belarus's streets throughout the year, and many of the most prominent voices were jailed by the Lukashenko administration.

Many people across the world wanted to donate to the Belarus protesters, but what mechanism could they use? No American banks would allow for wire transfers to a bank in Belarus. Even if an American bank did allow it, the Lukashenko administration would halt any transfers intended to aid protesters. Financial technology applications like Venmo, Cash App, and Zelle would not work either, as none of these apps allow sending money to Belarus. So, where could people turn to aid the protesters in their fight against an authoritarian regime?

The answer was Bitcoin. Hundreds of Belarus protesters and non-profit organizations posted Bitcoin addresses online for people worldwide to contribute donations. Think about the significance of this. Besides Bitcoin (and other cryptocurrencies, all of which are derived from Bitcoin's technological breakthroughs), there was not a single method in the world to donate to those in Belarus. This is censorship resistance, and it highlights the value of decentralized digital money that does not require any intermediaries to transact. Over $500,000 was donated to BYSOL, a grassroots Belarusian human rights organization, all in Bitcoin.[58]

There are countless examples throughout the world of groups of people who cannot trust their own native currencies. It is the norm, not the exception, which is a dissonance that many Americans face when trying to understand the concept of a currency that does not come from a government. In America, we have always been able to rely on the dollar—though remember, gold was the backbone of America's currency until 1971—and this has led us to spend our lives without taking the time to even think about how money works at all. This is an enormous privilege. It can be difficult for an American to understand the "why" of Bitcoin. For someone in Argentina, Lebanon, or Venezuela, however, they understand it immediately.

Censorship resistance is not about breaking rules; it is about neutrality. It is about designing a system that is not capable of being corrupted. Bitcoin's censorship resistance, combined with its fixed monetary policy and decentralization, represents the first neutral and apolitical money that has ever existed. Having more Bitcoin does not allow you to change the rules to get your way, as money works today in our current system. In Bitcoin, the most powerful person in the world and the least powerful are treated the same.

These three properties—decentralization, monetary soundness, and censorship resistance—join together to create a distributed and open money unlike any that has ever existed before. For the first time in history, there now is a form of money that cannot be corrupted. The rules were set once at the start, and now they are set in stone.

BITCOIN VERSUS FIAT MONEY

CONTRAST THIS APPROACH with how our modern fiat money works, where money is used as a political tool. Transferring and measuring value has become just one of many roles that money plays today. This perversion of the role of money, which occurs through manipulating the money supply, is the direct cause of the many societal issues discussed in length throughout the Modern Money section of this book.

When the supply of money cannot be manipulated, money maintains its true purpose—to measure value and transfer it through space and time. Modern money has destroyed the ability to save money through time because of inflation, which has led to the tremendous debt crisis, distorted markets, and rising inequality that we see today.

At the moment, Bitcoin is still a risk for most people, particularly in the short term. Bitcoin has only existed for eleven years, and its value is very volatile (although trending up over time). The volatility is a result of the network being so small in the global scheme of things. As of this writing, the Bitcoin network has a market capitalization of $650 billion, which is less than 10% of the size of gold.

While that may sound large, compared to other currencies and financial assets Bitcoin is a small fish in the global financial system. This means that it takes less money buying and selling to significantly sway the price in either direction. Since most people still do not understand what Bitcoin is or how it works, the price will continue to be highly volatile until it reaches its eventual market saturation point.

It is easy for people to ascribe a narrative for what Bitcoin is. For most, they judge it by its price. Price is the least important part of how Bitcoin works, however, and should be the last thing that any individual tries to understand. Price is a distraction, and by getting caught up in the price of Bitcoin, people fail to consider what Bitcoin actually is.

Bitcoin is a natively digital money with a fixed supply. That is all that it is. It is wholly apolitical and neutral on its own. When people attempt to give Bitcoin a narrative, it is a sign that they do not understand what it is they are critiquing. Yet, being apolitical is itself a political statement. Bitcoin allows its users to opt out of the entire fiat money system. Instead of fighting over ways to change the current system, Satoshi Nakamoto created an alternative.

People will continue to say that Bitcoin is too volatile to work. They want the stability of the dollar. Users of Bitcoin take the opposite approach. While the price of Bitcoin is volatile, the protocol is incredibly stable, with the rules having stayed the same since its inception. When you hold Bitcoin, you know with certainty that your money will never be devalued through the issuance of new units, the way that fiat money works.

While fiat money has its policies decided in closed-door meetings conducted by central bankers, Bitcoin's monetary policy is fixed and has been available to the public from day one. Focusing on the price is the wrong approach. Instead, focus on the protocol itself. How volatile are the policies and rules of the system? In this way, Bitcoin is the stable and cautious approach, while modern fiat money takes the unreliable approach to policy.

Part of what makes Bitcoin interesting is that there has never been a monetary asset where the have-nots have gotten in before the elites. New Bitcoin have been mined since 2009, and because Bitcoin had little value for years; the coins exchanged hands freely—mostly among computer nerds and sound money advocates, in the early going. Even in 2017, when the price briefly spiked to $20,000, the wealthiest Americans were not interested, dismissing Bitcoin as a fad. Only in 2020, after eighteen million of the total twenty-one million Bitcoin had been mined, have the very first Wall Street types become interested.

Only a very few on Wall Street have Bitcoin so far, but it is likely a trend that will continue. There are an estimated one hundred million Bitcoin holders globally, the vast majority of whom are ordinary people who became interested and chose to acquire some. If Bitcoin's price rises significantly higher, Bitcoin will represent the most significant transfer of wealth from the "haves" to the "have-nots" in modern history. The little guy has never been able to front-run the big guy on this scale before Bitcoin.

The exact degree of Bitcoin's long-term success remains to be seen. There will no doubt be hurdles in its way. Still, trust in institutions continues to erode. Bitcoin requires no trust, which is part of its appeal. Even if Bitcoin does not reach its full potential as a currency, it will always be a noteworthy experiment. By showing the world that a decentralized currency is possible, Bitcoin has spawned thousands of imitators and other cryptocurrencies, many of which further explore the possibilities of what decentralized protocols can achieve.

CENTRAL BANK
DIGITAL CURRENCIES

T HE WORLD IS becoming increasingly digital, yet it is rare for the average American to consider the digitization of money. As it stands today, the modern banking system was built nearly half a century ago and runs on technology that is as outdated as the first Macintosh computer. While modern banking is technologically ancient, it is rarely questioned since there have not been feasible alternatives. However, beginning with the invention of Bitcoin, the possibilities of what digital money might mean for the future have become clearer. More than a decade after Bitcoin's first block was mined, central banks worldwide have begun to grasp the possibility of a truly digital currency.

DIGITAL BANKING – TODAY AND TOMORROW

FIRST, IT IS important to consider how money works today, as it is already digital. Less than 10% of the world's money is in the form of paper bills. The rest lies on bank balance sheets. In the 2000s, commerce was increasingly done using credit and debit cards, which are themselves a form of digital money. Our money is essentially just an entry in a digital accounting ledger by a bank, where banks simply add to and decrease the numbers in depositor's accounts. The system is archaic, however, built over decades and centuries and is in desperate need of an overhaul in the information age.

To understand just how severe the modern banking system's inadequacies are, consider the difficulties involved in sending a wire transfer or Automated Clearing House Network (ACH) payment. To send an ACH, you need both the recipient's account and routing numbers—both lengthy. Once you approve the transfer with your banking institutions, it could take a few days or more for the transfer to be processed by both banks and for the funds to be in the recipient's accounts. In an age where digital messages and information can be transferred from person to person instantly, there is no excuse for monetary transfers requiring more than a day.

Furthermore, the only reason paychecks are often issued by employers on a biweekly basis is due to the difficulty the modern banking structure imposes. Digital payments present significant efficiency improvements in this regard. Instead of being paid every other week for your labor, imagine being paid for your work by the second. This is only one of the many possibilities for money as we shift away from the archaic system that currently exists into a future powered by new technology.

A central bank digital currency (CBDC) would operate in a fashion that resembles Venmo and Cash App more than the banking system that stands today. Each user would have a wallet application, accessible either by mobile application or computer, that could receive deposits and send out payments for transactions. The difference is that instead of linking Venmo or Cash App to a bank to transfer funds, the Venmo-like app itself would be your own personal bank account with the Federal Reserve, able to receive direct deposits and transfer money quickly and efficiently.

The specifics of how this system would be implemented remain to be seen, since the Federal Reserve would not want to put all regional banks out of business. They will likely find a way to keep these banks involved as an unnecessary intermediary, but with a CBDC, a bank is not necessarily needed. Each user would have their own wallet/account directly with the central bank that would have the ability to receive paychecks directly, pay for milk at the grocery store, and send money to friends just as easily as could be done with Venmo.

THE PROS AND CONS OF CBDCS

To FURTHER EXPLORE the potential for money in a CBDC world, let us consider tax payment. In the digital age, there is little reason for a tax system that requires the level of time and effort that currently exists in the US. Now and again, you have likely heard someone say, "The government already knows how much we make. Could they not simply tell us how much is owed in taxes?"

Alas, it is not so in the current banking system. There are too many moving parts, too many different actors, and too much coordination that would be required by the IRS to handle the taxes of all Americans themselves. With a central bank digital currency, however, the calculus changes.

Since a CBDC involves a direct account link to the nation's central bank and government, these issuing bodies would have a direct level of access to American's finances in a way that is far beyond what exists today. If a CBDC was the national currency, not only could taxes be automatically calculated, but they could be automatically deducted from user accounts. The time-consuming process of calculating taxes each year would be eliminated, along with the headache that comes with it.

While this sounds appealing, and in many ways is, there are numerous ways in which a central bank digital currency can potentially oppress its users' rights. This can be seen in China, which will likely be the country to launch the first true central bank digital currency. There have been rumors for years about China's plan to launch a digital currency, with an increasing number of leaks about the system's technical specifications over the past two years. China has minimized the use of cash heavily in recent years, with most payments in most areas using the WeChat application.

WeChat, a multi-purpose app that combines messaging features with social media, payment functions, and more, was launched in 2011 by Chinese technology behemoth Tencent Holdings and is used by nearly all Chinese citizens daily. According to CNBC, in 2019, WeChat boasted over one billion monthly users.[59] WeChat is also surveillance software for the authoritarian Chinese government.

With the level of use that WeChat has in China, combined with the nation's state-run economy, the Chinese government is responsible for the oppression of over a billion people. As previously noted, throughout the Free Hong Kong movement and protests throughout 2019, citizens who used their WeChat app to pay for metro fare to attend protests were later tracked and arrested. The same is true for groups who used the messaging features of WeChat to organize with one another in support of the protests.

Knowing that WeChat messaging was under surveillance, civilians flooded to lengthy lines at the cash-operated metro stations, even though those machines were previously scarcely used. There is no doubt that when China launches its central bank digital currency, it will be used for increasingly nefarious purposes. This is the downside of a digital national currency. There is a strong potential for abuse.

With a central bank digital currency, a user does not ever truly own their own money. When you own a cell phone, that phone is in your physical possession. While our own banking system today is digital in many ways, analog cash still exists. In digital form, our money stored in banks is an IOU, essentially a promise that users can withdraw funds if they choose. Users do not own their money when it is in the banking system. They hold a promise. With cash, you own the money itself.

Though banks do freeze accounts now, with a CBDC, a government would be able to freeze and seize depositor funds much more easily. With essentially the press of a button, a user's entire financial capability could be put to an immediate halt if suspected of a crime. If you get a parking ticket and missed the court date, that ticket payment could just be taken from your account. With a CBDC, there is no mechanism to prevent the seizure of funds. Contrast this to Bitcoin, which, while digital, is owned solely by the user in control of the private keys with no possibility for automatic seizure or frozen funds.

While it is fair to believe that a central bank digital currency would not be used to its full authoritarian potential in the West, it is imperative to understand that the potential for abuse is there. The only way for a CBDC to avoid these negative traits would be if the system were specifically designed so that no central bank or government could seize funds or freeze accounts. This is highly unlikely to occur, however, since privacy has been increasingly vilified in modern society. Surely the government would demand the ability to prevent payments to bad actors and terrorists, acting under the guise of national security.

As long as a system of money can freeze the accounts of terrorists, citizens' accounts could also be frozen if a bad actor came into power within the United States. Remember, a system of money is supposed to be neutral, a means of valuing goods. By restricting who can and who cannot participate in a system of value, the functions of money become perverted. It ends up being another manipulated political tool, which often results in harm to its users. History has demonstrated many times that if any system *can* be corrupted, eventually it will be.

Think about how, in 2020, President Trump declared the political protest movement Antifa to be a terrorist group due to violence that erupted during Black Lives Matter protests. While there was some violence at many of the demonstrations, the cause of the violence was not always clear.

The meaningful point here is that the president could arbitrarily define a hard-to-pinpoint group of Americans as engaging in terrorism. That designation put hundreds of thousands of Americans at risk of being excluded from the banking system. Banks are already quick to deny financial access to those in legal industries, such as cannabis sales, gambling, and sex work. Restricting the ability for a person to participate in banking at all is extremely dangerous. It forces people to hold money in cash, making them more likely to be victims of a crime.

While the current banking system does allow for account closures, a CBDC makes the process much more trivial. Under a CBDC system, any individual that President Trump believed to be a member of Antifa, a group with no formal membership, could have access to their finances frozen at any minute with the quick press of a few computer keys. There does not need to be an arrest warrant or a court order; simple suspicion is enough to freeze a person's life savings while an investigation is conducted. Central bank digital currencies offer numerous improvements over the modern system, but with the trade-off that a CBDC is more prone to abuse and corruption than even the current financial system.

As for other ways that a CBDC would allow for new possibilities within monetary policy, look no further than interest rates. Interest rates have steadily dropped throughout the last fifty years and have reached a point where rates globally are either nearly zero or negative. Interest rates affect two different aspects of the banking experience for most: borrowing and saving.

For a borrower, the lower the interest rate, the better, as the interest rate is the additional amount that a borrower needs to repay the bank for a loan. If a person takes out a one-year, $10,000 loan with a 5% interest rate, they will need to repay $10,500 at the end of the year. The lower the interest rate, the less the borrower needs to repay. With a negative interest rate, a borrower must repay a sum that is less than the original total borrowed. If the borrower were able to secure a rate of *negative* 5% in the above example, they would only need to repay $9,500 at the end of their loan term, essentially receiving $500 in free money due to taking out a loan. Because of this, negative interest rates heavily induce people to take out loans.

The flip side of the borrower, however, is the saver. Instead of going into debt by taking out loans, the saver prefers to keep their money in the bank where there is no risk of default. As discussed throughout this book, the modern economy has penalized savers through the exponential creation of new currency over the last fifty years, which has occurred alongside interest rates continuously trending downward. The opportunity cost of saving has expanded dramatically, as those individuals who have chosen to invest rather than save have seen tremendous growth in the valuations of equities and real estate, as the trillions of new dollars that have been printed flow into comparatively scarce financial assets. In other words, it costs money to save.

Negative interest rates take this to an entirely different degree. With negative rates, a depositor will have to pay the bank to store their savings, the reverse of the current system where the bank pays the depositor annual interest. With a negative 5% rate, $10,000 in savings would be reduced to $9,500 at the end of the year. In the same way that negative interest rates help the borrower, they penalize the saver.

Even though the steady drop in interest rates has led to a heavy incentive to invest and borrow instead of save, negative rates take this much further. By imposing an actual dollar cost to store wealth in the bank, depositors will become even more likely to keep as little cash in the bank as possible. This will lead to more debt on both the individual and national level, continued growth in inequality between the wealthy and the poor, higher prices for goods that do not benefit from the deflationary effects of technology, and an increasingly fragile economy that has become reliant on debt to function.

Negative interest rates are already in place in much of the world. As of December 2020, there is $18 trillion of negative rate yielding debt in countries around the world.[60] The Federal Reserve has claimed that they are not considering taking rates negative, but they will likely do so eventually. Rates are already near zero, and any attempt to raise rates even slightly in previous years has seen a vehement rejection from markets.

Simultaneously, there remains the need for continued

quantitative easing and other Fed programs to keep financial markets propped up. With interest rates already at zero, the Fed will eventually bring rates into the negative to stimulate the economy further. The reason they cannot do that in the near term, however, is primarily the existence of cash.

There is a direct link between countries that have reduced the use of cash and the ones with negative interest rates. Countries with low cash usage rates, such as Denmark, Japan, Sweden, and Switzerland, also own negative-yielding debt. While the US has certainly seen cash usage drop, there is still a sizable portion of the population that uses cash for small, everyday transactions. In countries where cash is still used regularly, it becomes much more difficult to impose negative interest rates. If depositors were forced to pay to keep their savings in the bank, many would rush to the banks to withdraw their savings to keep in cash.

A central bank digital currency would allow for the eventual elimination of cash in any given country. After China, Europe will likely be the next major region to institute a CBDC, a possibility which the European Central Bank (ECB) has already confirmed they are exploring.[61] When discussing the potential for a natively digital sovereign currency, it is common to hear central banks claim that any new CBDC will work in conjunction with cash and that the two systems will work in parallel with each other. This is unlikely to be true for very long. As long as cash continues to exist, central banks cannot enact the growing level of control that they deem necessary for their currencies. Negative interest rates can only work as long as there is no superior alternative.

CASH WOULD BE ILLEGAL IF INVENTED TODAY

IF IT WERE invented today, cash would never be legal. Although cash is how money has been used throughout nearly all of history, cash presents numerous problems for governments. The largest so-called issue is that cash cannot be tracked, surveilled, or electronically confiscated. To governments, this is a problem. For users, it is a feature.

While politicians like to claim that constant tracking, surveillance, and monitoring is a necessary measure for national security in the information age, financial privacy is a right that nearly all human rights organizations support. As shown earlier with China, financial surveillance is often used to oppress and control entire populations. Using a more universal example, financial control is a tool that is often used by those in abusive relationships. A controlling husband who does not let his wife have a bank account of her own has immense power in the relationship.

Finally, CBDCs offer the potential for new kinds of fiscal policy actions by the government, such as implementing a form of Universal Basic Income (UBI). Since Andrew Yang, 2020 Democratic presidential primary candidate, brought this concept into the discussion in the US, it has been thrust into mainstream conversation with the prospect of recurring stimulus checks throughout the COVID-19 pandemic. The odds of some form of UBI being implemented within the next decade or two has gone from a ludicrous proposition to quite possible.

Here is an example of how we can use our newfound knowledge of how money works to understand a political issue.

Simply put, any form of UBI would significantly expand

the money supply. If 350 million Americans received $1,000 a month, the total cost of $4.2 trillion would nearly equal the $4.45 trillion federal budget from 2019. The effects of this much currency entering the system would take the many issues that have cropped up over the last fifty years—rising inequality, distorted markets, and increasing costs in essential industries such as healthcare and college tuition—and make them significantly worse.

If the root cause of many of these issues is the massive amount of currency that has been created over the last century, UBI is more of a problem than a solution. When one-time $1,200 checks were issued to millions of Americans during the COVID-19 pandemic, the stock market soared in the following weeks and months. Americans who were affected by the pandemic spent their stimulus payments on food and necessities, while those that kept their jobs invested the money into financial assets, and the gap between the two groups grew. This is the problem with UBI in a nutshell. While it can be argued that the growth in inequality would be worth it, since millions of people could then afford necessities, the drastic increase in income inequality that would occur must be considered.

Central bank digital currencies are inevitable. With the current structure of the banking system operating on old and outdated rails, CBDCs represent the next evolution of fiat money. The path to a CBDC future is unclear, but the direction that money is heading is not. While CBDCs present numerous improvements over the current banking structure, they also present many ways in which money can continue to be used as a tool to manipulate and control.

While most of us do not realize it, money is intended to be neutral. It is not supposed to be able to choose sides. Money lets us measure value and, just as importantly, store that value over time. Throughout history, many different currencies have broken when minting bodies have issued more currency as a means to achieve some political goal. It is important to realize that it does not matter what the goal is, the impact on the currency is the same. Whether a king is creating more fiat money to enrich himself or a legislative branch of Congress is enacting a stimulus package to help those who have lost their jobs during the pandemic, *the effect on the currency is the same.*

When the purpose of money itself becomes political, a means to choose who may benefit and who may not, the entire system becomes structurally weaker. This is seen in our fragile economy today, which can no longer stay afloat without ever more debt. Money is now more political than at any time in modern history. Central bank digital currencies will make that specific problem worse. Regardless, CBDCs are coming. Though it may take another decade for such a system to be implemented in the US, it will happen eventually, and it is important to understand the benefits as well as the costs.

A FRAGILE SYSTEM

A s we reach the final section of *The Story of Money*, you have a much better understanding of money than you did at the start.

We discussed what money is and what separates good forms of money from bad forms of money, including the five properties: divisibility, durability, portability, recognizability, and scarcity. We looked through and studied money's entire history to learn lessons from its evolution.

We investigated how our modern system of money works and learned that it is more flawed, with more trade-offs to its design, than most people have realized. We saw how the modern monetary system will lead to more debt for the individual and the nation, a continually widening gap in inequality between the wealthy and the poor, higher prices for goods that do not benefit from the deflationary effects of technology, and an increasingly fragile economy that becomes reliant on debt to function.

Finally, we looked into the future of money and how it will function as an application layer in a way that has not existed before. As money becomes increasingly digital, we will see a battle between open and decentralized systems like Bitcoin and tightly controlled systems like central bank digital currencies (CBDCs).

Modern money is a house of cards. It is fragile. In political discussions, the arguments are about who gets to spend the money and on what. The conversation is never about how money gets created in the first place.

Instead, we blame whoever our political opponent is for how they are spending the money. We say that *how* they are spending the money is causing our problems, when a closer look reveals that the source of many issues is the money itself and the effects that occur when currency issuance becomes politicized. If America was a tree, much of politics is complaining about the branches, while the true problem is the root of the tree itself, the actual system of money.

Frankly, this may be too late to fix. The house of cards has gotten so high and is so wobbly and delicate that trying to wind it down may knock it over, and the system would collapse. There is also no real incentive for any politician to want less money in the world. The modern system of money benefits politicians above all else. More money created means more money to enact an agenda, at any cost.

It can also be argued that all the trade-offs that are associated with the modern system of money are worth it and that it is best for the country—and the world, since the current system of money is not US-specific—to accept these compromises because they allow society to progress and develop faster than we would otherwise. That is a valid point of view.

Most people are not aware that there are even trade-offs with how the modern system of money works; however, they are significant.

The dollar is simply a poor store of value, designed to lose value every year, which is uncomfortable to grapple with. This will continue as deficit spending becomes even further popularized, and politicians begin to believe that new programs do not need to be financed by tax revenue and the money can simply be printed.

At the beginning of this book, when we asked, "What

really is money, anyway?" we considered the three functions of money: unit of account, medium of exchange, and store of value. The dollar functions well for the first two, but it penalizes you for saving through inflation and is getting increasingly worse at storing value. Recognizing this dynamic gives you a significant advantage in understanding the economic machinations at play in our fragile financial system, in a way that goes far beyond the basic surface-level debates that we find on social media or the news. The awareness that money affects everything is a form of enlightenment. Once you start to understand, there is no going back.

MONEY AND TIME

SINCE MONEY AFFECTS everything, it is easy to lose the thread a bit, focus on the granular, and miss the big picture. The most prominent effect at play here is the erosion of the store of value function of money. It is the failure of the dollar—and all fiat money—to maintain its value throughout the years that has resulted in the debt-driven, investment-obsessed, distorted-markets economy that the world now finds itself in.

Storing value goes beyond simply saving money, however. It is more cosmic than that. Saving money is not just saving value, it is also saving time itself.

Most of us have heard the expression that time is money. This is entirely backward.

When people say that time is money, they mean that instead of wasting time, you should do something productive and make money. But why do we want to make money in the first place? And what does it mean when we do earn money?

Time is the scarcest resource that there is. There is only

moving forward in time, no going back. When most people think about money, they get caught up in the day-to-day. They have bills to pay, food to buy, goods that they want, and they need to earn money to get those things. Even when they are thinking about the future, such as saving for a house or retirement, they are not considering the role that money plays in storing time itself and how that function of money is being distorted by how the modern system of money works.

When a person goes to work and gets paid for an eight-hour shift, that means that they were paid for the labor that was provided. That person gave up their time to earn that money. In essence, eight hours of time was converted and is now being stored in the form of money. The money represents actual time spent working.

The way that money should work—and how money does work when it is a good store of value—is that the value it represents should not significantly depreciate over time. If someone works for eight hours in 2021, if they are paid for eight hours of time, that money should still be worth eight hours of time in the future.

But it is not. And that is because of inflationary money.

Imagine a person who works for eight hours a day in 2021 and is compensated with $120. Due to inflation, $120 will not buy as much in 2031 as it does in 2021. With 2% inflation a year, which is what the Federal Reserve aims for, $120 will buy about 25% less in 2031 than it does today. If a person worked eight hours in 2020 and keeps it in the bank for ten years, eight hours of work is now worth just six hours of work because of the 25% drop in purchasing power.

Think about that again—what was earned for eight hours of time is now only worth six hours of time just ten years later. This means that two hours of time that have already been worked have essentially been stolen because of inflation.

It is not uncommon to occasionally hear people wonder, "Why are we still working forty hours a week? We have the most advanced technology we have ever had and produce more goods than ever. Why do we still need to work eight hours a day?" The reason is that the value of productive time already worked vanishes into thin air because of inflation. Even with just 2% inflation, 25% of money's purchasing power disappears over the course of ten years. Doubling that means that essentially 50% of what a worker saves today, along with the time spent earning it, will be gone in twenty years if that money is just being saved in the bank.

The reason that it is necessary to need to work until the age of sixty-five or seventy is that in our later years, we are re-earning the money that was lost to inflation over decades. If a person spends eight hours working in their twenties and saves the payment for that work in the bank, that money will have lost more than 90% of its value after fifty years. This means that working eight hours at the age of twenty is worth essentially nothing at the age of seventy, all because the money did such a bad job of storing the time that was spent earning it. Now, people need to work into their sixties to catch up on all the lost value from decades prior, which was taken away due to inflation.

Money is how we store time. When you hear that money is supposed to hold value, what that means is that if you spend eight hours working and are paid money for that work, the money should still be worth eight hours of time in the future.

That is not how money works today though. Instead, the hours that we spend working lose nearly all their value overs decades.

ADOPTING A MULTICURRENCY MINDSET

AMERICANS ARE USED to just thinking in dollar terms. The dollar is the strongest currency in the world; therefore, we can use the dollar for everything. This is not the reality in countries around the world, however. For people in most nations, the local currency cannot be relied on to store value over time. If you look at many global currencies, like the Nicaraguan cordoba or the Pakistani rupee, the value of the money consistently falls against the US dollar over a long period.

People in these countries are used to thinking with a multicurrency mindset. They understand that they cannot store wealth in their local currency. Because of this, they hold different currencies for different purposes. For regular day-to-day spending, they will use their local currency. For saving money, they will try to acquire US dollars to the extent that they can.

It is not always easy to acquire dollars, however. People in many nations cannot simply open a US dollar bank account in a lot of these countries, which is an issue, but the takeaway is that these people try to acquire dollars whenever they can. Their multicurrency mindset is to spend in the local currency which everyone accepts, but save in a currency that stores value over time, and for these people, that has traditionally been the US dollar.

Now, in America—or Europe, Japan, Switzerland or concerning one of the other strong currencies around the world—it is uncommon to think this way. Since these are already the strongest currencies, we cannot use them for both spending and saving?

As discussed throughout this book, the answer is no. The US dollar is losing value every year from inflation. When inflation is 2% annually, you lose 25% of the purchasing power of your savings every ten years.

This loss of value through inflation is why there is the need to "make our money grow." In a way, Americans treat the stock market and their 401K the same way that someone in Nicaragua views the US dollar—as a tool for savings.

The stock market is not the same thing as saving, however; it is investing in a financial asset. This financialization of savings has become so normalized that the line between saving (avoiding risk) and investing (taking risk) have become blurred to such a degree that most people think the two are the same thing.

While this is certainly the conventional wisdom, it is not natural at all. It is not natural for money to lose purchasing power over time. Prices rising is a deliberate and political choice. Left to their own nature, prices would fall with the passage of time as human processes become more efficient and technology improves. Our central bank, and all modern central banks, have chosen a monetary structure where inflation occurs, and where money loses value.

Since Americans think that there is no currency alternative to run to, the way someone in Nicaragua runs to the US dollar, the standard practice is to treat financial assets as a savings mechanism. The result is the debt-ridden economic system that exists today, where everyone's retirement money is being stored in investments that were always supposed to be risky.

It does not matter that your Bitcoin cannot be spent in stores. Americans will learn to adopt a multicurrency mindset, the way so much of the world already has with how they acquire US dollars for saving. Different monies can be used for different purposes. The dollar is good for spending but lacks when it comes to saving.

If you want to store your wealth in a money that prioritizes saving, you need to look outside the dollar or any fiat currency, and that is where gold and Bitcoin start to look more valuable. When you compare the dollar, gold, and Bitcoin solely based on their properties as money—blocking out all the extra noise like politics—gold and Bitcoin excel with their store of value features, while the dollar sacrifices store of value in search of growth through inflation.

As global debt continues to grow and fiat money supply rises exponentially, people will begin to see that their savings are losing value and will naturally begin to gravitate towards the forms of money with the best store of value properties. This is the lesson from monetary history. It is likely to benefit both gold and Bitcoin.

While Bitcoin has certain risks that gold does not, since it has only existed for eleven years, it also carries numerous advantages over gold. It is even scarcer than gold, with a fixed 21 million cap. It can be transported across the globe almost instantly. There has never been a counterfeit Bitcoin. If you are knowledgeable enough about Bitcoin security, Bitcoin can be essentially impossible to steal and cannot be hacked.

THE BIG PICTURE

IT IS EASY to get lost in the weeds when thinking about the world. The details feel like the most important thing to focus on. There will always be a reason to say, "but what about...?"

The details are where we get confused, however. By focusing on the trees, we lose sight of the forest. Instead of looking from the perspective of an individual chess piece, it is necessary to consider the entire board and look at the big picture.

The primary purpose of *The Story of Money* is to get people to start thinking about how money works as a system.

People joke that money does not grow on trees, but the reality is that both in the US and throughout much of the world, many people do not ever think about how money "grows" at all.

We know that we each personally do not have enough money and that we wish we had more, and we complain and argue about how money gets used, but there is a disconnect between the desire for money and how the entire system affects everyday society. Since money is the base layer on which our civilization is built, our system of money profoundly affects everything that we do.

To put it simply, there is reason to be concerned about our modern system of money. Over the last fifty years, there has been unprecedented growth in productivity because of technological change, and on average quality of life has steadily improved alongside it. Not everything is for the better, however. Income inequality has been rising, widening the gap between the wealthy and the poor. Markets have been distorted, with many goods remaining cheap while other essential goods and services have gotten exponentially more expensive.

There is tension in the air, as both sides of the political aisle are as ideologically far apart as they have been in recent history. This book's thesis is that many of these societal problems can be explained by how modern money works and the effects it has on everyday life.

Money in the bank is losing value every year, and saving is heavily punished, encouraging risky investment. Large asset bubbles have been created, with the value of all financial assets climbing higher than ever. It is clear to many that these valuations may not be based on fundamentals, even to the observers who do not fully understand the mechanics behind the valuations. Still, everyone participates anyway because simply saving dollars in the bank is a guaranteed way to fall behind.

When the music is on, you need to dance. This is what happens when there is no restriction on the amount of new money that can be created and the power of the currency printing press is used for political purposes.

Money does not store value anymore, however, and holding cash is penalized. Most of the population recognizes this without understanding it. They know that they needed their money to grow over time, and so they invest in their 401k and the stock market. It is practically second nature to most people. They do not even think about it. They do not realize that this is the financialization of the economy and what it represents is a failure of the dollar to hold value. Since the dollar cannot capably hold value throughout the years, they must search for alternative methods to store their purchasing power.

As time has gone by and new currency has been exponentially created, the economy has become increasingly financialized. "Making your money grow" has become a common mantra of the people, understood as the only method to meaningfully hold wealth over time. This results from the conditioning that it is normal for money to lose time, which is contrary to progress and the natural gravitation of monetary history. Individuals have always naturally been attracted to the forms of money that best held their value, and the civilizations that followed this mindset thrived.

Saving and investing are not meant to be the same thing, though that is how they are treated today. Saving money in the bank results in falling behind. Only by investing in financial assets can an individual maintain enough wealth to retire eventually.

MONEY AND POLITICS

THE FUTURE OF money is not something that can be changed by a vote or through politicians. It will be the same no matter which nation makes which choice; the only question is the direction and timeline to that endpoint. The path for how money will continue to develop has already been set. We need to think macro. This book is not an argument for a particular set of policies to fight for a specific future of money. Instead, this book is meant to show what is already happening, regardless of our choices and the politicians we elect.

The trend of printing more fiat money will continue at an increasing rate. Not only has the modern economy become dependent on a rapidly increasing money supply, but the Overton window—the range of policies politically acceptable to the mainstream population at a given time—has shifted among the public as well. Concerns about deficit spending are falling by the wayside.

The developing consensus is that to drive the country forward the Federal Reserve and the government must spend to get it there. And thus, spending will continue. As the money supply grows, the problems resulting from that expansion will grow alongside the supply. First and foremost, this results in a tax on savings and the incentive for people to spend their incomes and go into debt.

This is the cause and effect that has led to a few different things. The penalty for saving pushes individuals to spend as much of their earnings as possible, leading to the significant appreciation of financial assets and real estate. The growth in these financial sectors does not mean the equities themselves produce any more value than they have in the past. Instead, the rise in the price of financial assets reflects the dollar's devaluation as the currency supply has significantly expanded.

At the same time, the poorest Americans are unable to partake in the investment of financial assets. They spend their money on necessities and typically save whatever they can in the form of cash in the bank, which is risk-free. However, risk-free does not mean safe, and the purchasing power of the money saved in the bank is falling each year. The result is that the poorest Americans are falling further behind since their savings are being devalued.

A critical point here is that it is simply the expansion of the money supply that causes this. While the money supply has always grown in the US, the rate of new dollars created since 1971 has far exceeded the currency issuance rates from prior decades and centuries. As noted earlier in the book, more dollars were created in June 2020 than in the first 200 years of the US dollar's existence. If this trend continues, which seems likely, the wealth gap between the rich and the poor will continue to grow.

No policy or tax can fix this because it is the natural mechanism of how the modern system of money works. Any policy that involves creating new money inherently results in increased inequality.

The continued expansion of the money supply will continue to distort market prices. Industries where technology is not advancing quickly enough to reduce costs will see their costs continue to rise, such as in healthcare and college tuition. While society will debate what to do about these rising costs, likely with no progress in today's hyper-partisan reality, the cause of these increasing prices will go undiscussed and misdiagnosed.

These skyrocketing costs reflect the devaluation of the dollar throughout the last five decades. The reason that not all industries have suffered from the same kind of cost increases is that technology has exponentially improved alongside the depreciating dollar. The deflationary impacts of technological improvement have countered the inflationary effects of currency creation, which has allowed most of what we produce to stay relatively low in cost.

The system cannot easily be rolled back either. While an inflationary system of money tends to encourage the users of that money to take on debt to fund investments, the system itself has become reliant on new money production. Tax revenue does not fully fund the government anymore, which means that the current level of government operation is dependent on new money entering circulation.

This is equally true of private enterprise, which has itself become reliant on low interest rates and cheap money. If it was decided that the amount of new money production was problematic and needed to be stopped, our entire economic system would break down. A system built on debt needs more and more debt to survive. That is the potentially unfixable flaw of modern money.

This leads to a difficult dilemma for any individual who understands the economic forces at play.

It is easy to support the idea of helping Americans who are in need. When we see that people are hungry or struggling to pay bills at the end of the month, it is a natural reaction to have that something needs to be done to help those people. The common refrain is that only the greed and self-interest of the wealthy prevent us from helping those who are less fortunate. As has been discussed here, however, that is not the only force at play.

Most Americans do not understand money, however, which was the primary motivation behind this book. Understanding what money is, its fundamental properties, and how a system of money affects life in ways that most do not realize reveals that printing too much money leads to societal consequences that range from mild to large enough that a country could collapse. It is a case where intention does not matter as much as the result, with policies designed to help those in need often resulting in the most harm. Comprehending money means knowing that aiding people today will result in greater inequality tomorrow. There is no right or wrong answer in this scenario.

The point here is not to sway you in one direction or the other. Instead, the purpose is to understand that there are trade-offs at play—significant ones—and that these trade-offs and second-order effects have consequences that must be considered carefully. Too much money in circulation risks hyperinflation, which devastates countries.

The other side of this spectrum is what happens if the government decides to halt spending immediately and run tax surpluses to reduce deficits and debt. Briefly, the results would be catastrophic to the economy. Since valuations have only reached their current levels due to cheap money in the form of debt, limiting new debt creation would likely result in a market collapse not seen in the lifespan of anyone alive today. An economy built on debt needs more and more debt to survive. To limit new currency issuance would be akin to a longtime drug addict being forced to go cold turkey to quit their addiction. The withdrawal would be fierce.

ARE WE MOVING FORWARD?

MONEY IS SUPPOSED to be neutral. It is not a tool to be wielded by the powerful. The purpose of money is to measure value and transfer that value through both space and time. At different points in history, money succeeded and failed at different parts of this equation.

Storing wealth through time was difficult, as most early forms of money were simply not scarce enough to maintain value. In this way, modern money is a step backward. Moving from gold to fiat was a choice between scarcity and convenience/control. The fact that gold is much less portable than fiat made the choice easy for individuals to accept once the final link between gold and paper money had been broken.

While it is unlikely that citizens in medieval times would have willingly accepted straight fiat money with no backing by gold, the mental link broke in people's minds over decades. If you grow up believing that money is paper, then it matters less whether the paper is backed by gold or if it is backed by the platitude of "the strength of a government."

When the dollar operated on a gold standard, the money supply still grew. Money was still inflationary on the gold standard. The importance of the gold standard is that there was a cap to the amount of new money that could be created. Money could not be created at will. While inflationary money can work if new currency issuance is kept low, removing the limit to the amount of new money has resulted in levels of money printing and spending that have resulted in the corruption of economies around the world.

It is inevitable that whoever has the power to print money will do so eventually. No amount of self-discipline can prevent this, as creating new currency is almost always in current politicians' best interests. This is a result of short-term thinking to achieve short-term goals.

When analyzing life today, much of what we see stems from the fact that we are not able to save using our money. After the constraint on the money supply was lifted by President Nixon in 1971, America began its march toward being the country that it finds itself as today. Since then, the money supply has expanded tenfold, and the country finds itself in a level of political turmoil that has not been seen in at least half a century.

Income inequality and the cost of essential goods and services have steadily increased over the last fifty years. Those at the bottom are struggling while stock markets are hitting all-time highs. While these appear to be opposite results, they are directly connected. The reason income inequality has risen is the same reason that stock prices keep going up. They are both symptoms of the same problem—a devaluing currency driven by money printing. Unfortunately, very few Americans understand the modern system of money and thus are not aware of its role in so many current political issues.

We can learn from the past that humanity has consistently trended towards the forms of money that store wealth the best over time. Holding wealth leads to a rise in innovation and standards of living. Remember how the early use of money allowed civilizations to focus on tasks other than solely farming for their survival?

Saving means consuming less than you produce, with the savings being stored in the form of money. If you cannot store wealth for a long time in a money, you cannot save, resulting in a lack of security and an inability to do works other than what is required for you to consume. If you are unable to save, all your effort must go into tasks that require short-term consumption. Good money changes this.

Newly armed with knowledge far beyond what you had before, you are now capable of recognizing the unbelievably important role that a system of money plays in society. Money affects everything, but those effects are not always obvious. Use this knowledge to better understand the world around you.

As they say, it always comes down to the money.

REFERENCES

1. Staff, Reuters. 2020. "Lebanon Inflation Soars above 100% Year-On-Year in July." *Reuters*, August 26, 2020. https://www.reuters.com/article/lebanon-crisis-inflation/lebanon-inflation-soars-above-100-year-on-year-in-july-idUSL8N2FS5TU.

2. Zeder, Melinda (October 2011). "The Origins of Agriculture in the Near East." Current Anthropology. 52 (S4): 221–235. doi:10.1086/659307. JSTOR 10.1086/659307.

3. Visualizing Human Geography, Second edition, Alyson L. Greiner[1119147565]

4. Doolin, A. (1985, July). Retrieved from https://web.archive.org/web/20090405172236/http://www.cowry.org/archive/NSN306CY.HTM

5. Gillilland, Cora Lee C. (1975). The Stone Money of Yap. A Numismatic Survey. (Smithsonian Studies in History and Technology 23). Washington, DC: Smithsonian Institution Press. p. 75.

6. Gelb, I. (2019, March 20). Sumerian language. Retrieved from https://www.britannica.com/topic/Sumerian-language

7. Hays, J. (2018, September). MESOPOTAMIAN ECONOMICS AND MONEY. Retrieved from http://factsanddetails.com/world/cat56/sub363/item1514.html

8. Bible Passages. (n.d.). Retrieved from https://biblehub.com/deuteronomy/25-13.htm

9. "China Ancient Currency, Shell Money before Qin Dynasty." 2016. Travelchinaguide.com. 2016. https://www.travelchinaguide.com/intro/focus/currency.htm.

10. "HISTORY of MONEY." 2019. Historyworld.net. 2019. http://www.historyworld.net/wrldhis/PlainTextHistories.asp?historyid=ab14.

11. Kurke, Leslie (1999). Coins, Bodies, Games, and Gold: The Politics of Meaning in Archaic Greece. Princeton University Press. pp. 6–7. ISBN 0691007365.

12. Cartwright, Mark. 2016. "Ancient Greek Coinage." Ancient History Encyclopedia. Ancient History Encyclopedia. July 15, 2016. https://www.ancient.eu/Greek_Coinage/.

13. As estimated by L. Migeotte, L'Économie des cités grecques, p. 55.

14. Renfrew, Sir Colin (1972). The Emergence of Civilisation: The Cyclades and the Aegean in The Third Millennium BC, p. 280.

15. "Trade in Ancient Greece." Ancient History Encyclopedia. Ancient History Encyclopedia. May 22, 2018. https://www.ancient.eu/article/115/trade-in-ancient-greece/.

16. Christoff-Kurapovna, Marcia. 2017. "Cradles of Capitalism: The City-States of Greece and Italy." Mises Institute. November 3, 2017. https://mises.org/wire/cradles-capitalism-city-states-greece-and-italy.

17. Mark, Joshua J. 2009. "Ancient Rome." Ancient History Encyclopedia. September 2, 2009. https://www.ancient.eu/Rome/.

18. Cartwright, Mark. 2018. "Roman Coinage." Ancient History Encyclopedia. April 19, 2018. https://www.ancient.eu/Roman_Coinage/.

19. "Roman Coins | UNRV.com." 2019. Unrv.com. 2019. https://www.unrv.com/economy/roman-coins.php.

20. "The Roman Empire: A Brief History." n.d. Milwaukee Public Museum. https://www.mpm.edu/research-collections/anthropology/anthropology-collections-research/mediterranean-oil-lamps/roman-empire-brief-history.

21. Butcher, Kevin. n.d. "Debasement and the Decline of Rome." https://warwick.ac.uk/fac/arts/classics/intranets/staff/butcher/debasement_and_decline.pdf.

22. School of Archaeology, University of Oxford https://web.archive.org/web/20080716025330/http://web.arch.ox.ac.uk/coins/cci8.htm. Archived from the original on July 16, 2008.

23. "مبتعث للدراسات والاستشارات الاكاديمية." n.d. Www.mobt3ath.com. https://www.mobt3ath.com/uplode/book/book-23488.pdf.

24. Pamuk, Şevket, and Maya Shatzmiller. 2014. "Plagues, Wages, and Economic Change in the Islamic Middle East, 700–1500." The Journal of Economic History 74 (1): 196–229. https://doi.org/ 10.1017/s0022050714000072.

25. "Economic Achievements." 2019. The Golden Age of Islam. 2019. https://golden-age-of-islam.weebly.com/economic-achievements.html.

26. "Why the Arabic World Turned Away from Science." 2011. The New Atlantis. 2011. https://www.thenewatlantis.com/ publications/why-the-arabic-world-turned-away-from-science.

27. Ebrey; Walthall; Palais (2006). East Asia: A Cultural, Social, and Political History. Boston: Houghton Mifflin Company. ISBN 978-0-6181-3384-0.

28. "Chinese Paper Money." 2018. Silk Road. 2018. http://www.silk-road.com/artl/papermoney.shtml.

29. "The Decline of Feudalism." n.d. https://www.roxbury.org/cms/ lib07/NJ01912906/Centricity/Domain/413/chapter-5.pdf.

30. Philip Daileader, The Late Middle Ages, audio/video course produced by The Teaching Company, (2007) ISBN 978-1-59803-345-8.

31. Cartwright, Mark. 2020. "The Hundred Years' War: Consequences & Effects." Ancient History Encyclopedia. March 6, 2020. https://www.ancient.eu/article/1520/the-hundred-years-war-consequences--effects/.

32. "How Banks Create Money—Positive Money." 2013. Positive Money. 2013. https://positivemoney.org/how-money-%20works/how-banks-%20create-money/.

33. Davies, Glyn, A History of Money, From Ancient Times to the Present Day, University of Wales Press 1994.

34. Szabo, Nick. 2002. "Shelling Out: The Origins of Money | Satoshi Nakamoto Institute." Nakamotoinstitute.org. 2002. https://nakamotoinstitute.org/shelling-out/.

35. Tweedy, Ann. n.d. "From Beads to Bounty: How Wampum Became America's First Currency." Indian Country Today. https://indiancountrytoday.com/archive/from-beads-to-bounty-

how-wampum-became-america-s-first-currency-76Ql3IPA2kKpBqfHiggjXw.

36. Glyn Davies. 2007. "A History of Money: From Ancient Times to the Present Day." http://library.uniteddiversity.coop/Money_and_Economics/A_History_of_Money-From_Ancient_Times_to_the_Present_Day.pdf.

37. "History of United States Currency | MyCreditUnion.gov." n.d. Www.mycreditunion.gov. https://www.mycreditunion.gov/financial-resources/history-united-states-currency.

38. Glyn Davies. 2007. "A History of Money: From Ancient Times to the Present Day." http://library.uniteddiversity.coop/Money_and_Economics/A_History_of_Money-From_Ancient_Times_to_the_Present_Day.pdf.

39. Board of Governors of the Federal Reserve System (U.S.), and Federal Reserve Board. 1989. "June 1989." Federal Reserve Bulletin, June. https://fraser.stlouisfed.org/title/federal-reserve-bulletin-62/june-1989-20805?start_page=3.

40. Salerno, Joseph. 2019. "Money and Gold in the 1920s and 1930s: An Austrian View." Mises Institute. June 11, 2019. https://mises.org/wire/money-and-gold-1920s-and-1930s-austrian-view.

41. Tassava, Christopher. 2002. "The American Economy during World War II." Eh.net. 2002. https://eh.net/encyclopedia/the-american-economy-during-world-war-ii/.

42. "Historical Inflation Rates: 1914-2019." 2019. US Inflation Calculator. April 10, 2019. https://www.usinflationcalculator.com/inflation/historical-inflation-rates/.

43. "United States Fed Funds Rate | 2019 | Data | Chart | Calendar | Forecast." 2019. Tradingeconomics.com. 2019. https://tradingeconomics.com/united-states/interest-rate.

44. "Federal Debt: Total Public Debt as Percent of Gross Domestic Product." 2019. Stlouisfed.org. 2019. https://fred.stlouisfed.org/series/GFDEGDQ188S.

45. "United States Money Supply M2 | 1959-2020 Data | 2021-2022 Forecast | Historical." n.d. Tradingeconomics.com. https://tradingeconomics.com/united-states/money-supply-m2.

46. "United States Fed Funds Rate | 2019 | Data | Chart | Calendar |

Forecast." 2019. Tradingeconomics.com. 2019.
https://tradingeconomics.com/united-states/interest-rate.

47. Diaz, Jesus. 2014. "If You Fold a Paper in Half 103 Times It'll Get
as Thick as the Universe." Gizmodo. July 14, 2014.
https://gizmodo.com/if-you-fold-a-paper-in-half-103-times-it-
will-be-as-thi-1607632639

48. Kandur, Jane Louise. 2017. "Stardust Is Gold Dust." Daily Sabah.
October 21, 2017. https://www.dailysabah.com/feature/2017/
10/21/stardust-is-gold-dust.

49. Dr. Elizabeth Cummins. 2015. "Tutankhamun's Tomb
(Innermost Coffin and Death Mask)—Smarthistory."
Smarthistory.org. 2015. https://smarthistory.org/tutankhamuns-
tomb-innermost-coffin-and-death-mask/.

50. Harper, Justin. 2020. "How Much Gold Is There Left to Mine in
the World?" BBC News, September 23, 2020, sec. Business.
https://www.bbc.com/news/business-54230737.

51. Board of Governors of the Federal Reserve System (US). 1980.
"M2 Money Stock." FRED, Federal Reserve Bank of St. Louis.
November 3, 1980. https://fred.stlouisfed.org/series/M2.

52. Ahmed, Saqib Iqbal. 2019. "U.S. Dollar Share of Global Currency
Reserves at Lowest since 2013: IMF Data." Reuters, September
30, 2019. https://www.reuters.com/article/us-forex-reserves/u-s-
dollar-share-of-global-currency-reserves-at-lowest-since-2013-
imf-data-idUSKBN1WF1IO.

53. Silver, Caleb. n.d. "The Top 20 Economies in the World."
Investopedia. https://www.investopedia.com/insights/worlds-
top-economies.

54. Hamilton, Isobel Asher. 2019. "WeChat Users in the US Say the
App Is Censoring Their Messages about Hong Kong—Business
Insider." Business Insider. November 26, 2019.
https://www.businessinsider.com/us-wechat-users-censored-
messages-hong-kong-china-2019-11.

55. "Wayback Machine." 2006. Web.archive.org. November 9, 2006.
https://web.archive.org/web/20061109161419/http://www.e-
gold.com/stats.html.

56. Wile, Rob. n.d. "How a Manhattan Jeweler Wound up with Gold
Bars Filled with Tungsten." Business Insider. Accessed January 30,

2021. https://www.businessinsider.com/tungsten-filled-gold-bars-found-in-new-york-2012-9.

57. Horn, Tina. How the Financial Sector Is Making Life Miserable For Sex Workers. https://www.vice.com/en/article/4w74jg/how-the-financial-sector-is-making-life-miserable-for-sex-workers-714

58. Gladstein, Alex. 2020 https://twitter.com/gladstein/status/1340836877595594752

59. Kharpal, Arjun. 2019. "Everything You Need to Know about WeChat—China's Billion-User Messaging App." CNBC. February 4, 2019. https://www.cnbc.com/2019/02/04/what-is-wechat-china-biggest-messaging-app.html.

60. Mullen, Cormac. 2020. "World's Negative-Yielding Debt Pile Hits $18 Trillion Record." Bloomberg.com, December 11, 2020. https://www.bloomberg.com/news/articles/2020-12-11/world-s-negative-yield-debt-pile-at-18-trillion-for-first-time.

61. Bank, European Central. 2020. "We Must Be Prepared to Issue a Digital Euro." Www.ecb.europa.eu, October. https://www.ecb.europa.eu/press/blog/date/2020/html/ecb.blog201002~12ab1c06b5.en.html.